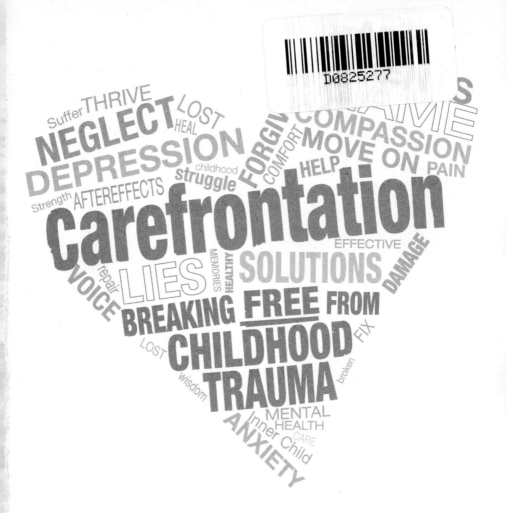

ARLENE DRAKE, PHD, MFT

Regan Arts.

NEW YORK

To my mother, Yolanda,
the woman who led the way for me
to become all I could be.

Regan Arts.

65 Bleecker Street
New York, NY 10012

Copyright © 2017 by Arlene Drake

All rights reserved, including the right to reproduce this book or portions thereof in any form whatsoever. For information, address Regan Arts Subsidiary Rights Department, 65 Bleecker Street, New York, NY 10012.

First Regan Arts hardcover edition, March 2017

Library of Congress Control Number: 2016955003

ISBN 978-1-942872-81-8

No one other than the author is identified by his or her real name in this book. Physical features and other potentially identifying characteristics also have been changed in many instances, and some characters and events are composites.

Interior design by Nancy Singer
Cover design by Richard Ljoenes

Printed in the United States of America

10 9 8 7 6 5 4 3 2 1

WITHDRAWN
FROM
COLLECTION

CONTENTS

WITHDRAWN FROM COLLECTION

INTRODUCTION

Imagine meeting a small child who's five or six. The little one cautiously approaches you and whispers, "I'm so scared. My mom has been hurting me," then turns around and gingerly lifts the back of a stained T-shirt. You immediately see the marks and bruises.

What do you do?

I can't think of anyone who wouldn't rush to comfort this little one, keep the child from danger, and find out what the hell is going on at home. It's obvious the child is helpless, in trouble, and needs protection. Parents or not, we instinctively know what to do: drop everything and take care of the child.

But what if that child is *you*?

I'm a psychotherapist specializing in trauma recovery, and that's the question I use to open the door to healing for adults whose lives have been damaged by the abuse they suffered as children. Every adult who was beaten, neglected, insulted, belittled, sexually assaulted, or otherwise abused in childhood carries the trauma inside. The traumatized child part of the self is vividly alive. Its experiences leave a lifelong imprint on both body and mind. And the most effective way I've found to recover from the effects abuse has left on your life is to work directly with the hurt child inside you.

You probably know, or strongly suspect, that something awful happened to you when you were small. No one lines up to see a

1

person who specializes in childhood abuse and trauma—or picks up a book like this—unless they've run out of other options, other therapies, other explanations for why their lives are so stuck and they still feel so bad.

This book is for you if you know or suspect you were abused—physically, sexually, or emotionally—or neglected as a child. It's also for you if you've struggled with depression, anger, or anxiety and never gotten to its root. You might not necessarily label your childhood "abusive," but you might describe life with your parents as "difficult" or "crazy" or "fucked up" and think it might be time to take another look at what went on—because every other explanation for the way you feel now has come up short.

You're probably not sure going back into it will help. Most people who were abused in some way as children have grown up trying to persuade themselves that the pain they experienced then is something most adults should have outgrown by now.

So they "put the past in perspective." Yes, they admit, things were tough when they were kids. Yes, even brutal at times. But that was a long time ago, and they tell themselves it makes sense to focus on the present not get bogged down in things that can't be changed. "My parents did the best they could under the circumstances, and what good could it possibly do to demonize them or dwell on what happened?" clients tell me. "Maybe, all things considered, it wasn't that bad." Most people want to lose any sense that they were, or are, "victims." They want to find some peace in forgiveness, and move on.

It's a very adult perspective, and it may help you cope with a nightmare of a past.

But it won't help you heal.

If you want to be more than a survivor, if you want to have the peaceful, centered life that's always been just out of reach, you'll have to stop justifying what happened to you. You'll need to look through the eyes of the lost, hurt, heartbroken kid who's been pushed aside each time you've said, "It wasn't so bad."

Most people who come to see me nod knowingly when I say that. Yet the abused kid they were is the last thing most smart, world-weary survivors want to think about. The whole idea of considering the experiences and needs of that injured figure from the past seems useless at best. What would be the point? Why go back to revisit some "inner child" when the outer adult is the one who needs help right now?

But it's the child inside who holds the elusive key to healing. And once my clients see a frightened little boy or girl—a child with their own face—asking for help, the image is hard to shake.

And so it is with you. Do you save the child or don't you? Can you really look into the eyes of the terrified or overwhelmed kid in the mirror and say, "Don't make a big deal of it. The people who beat you up or raped you or made you feel like you were nothing were doing the best they could"?

Do you tell the child inside you to shut up while you explain that the abusers were probably addicts or "under pressure" or abuse victims themselves? Or do you step to the child's defense? Faced with that choice, I believe you, like most people, will embrace the child within.

I'll help you do that, with a process I have used for more than three decades to help hundreds of people work with both their hearts and their heads to heal the deepest pain in their lives. We'll wade into the challenge of listening to and taking care of the hurt child inside, and step-by-step, I'll show you how to heal the wounds of a miserable childhood by coming to that child as a compassionate adult with the heart and mind and guts to rescue it, and show it how to grow up. It's the most challenging—and life-changing—work you will ever do.

Finding the courage to *care* for the child and *confront* the child's truth—that's the essence of the process, and why I think of what we're doing as carefrontation, a blending of those two vital tasks.

Carefrontation is your guide to breaking free from the lies, secrets, and shame of the past and reclaiming your genuine self. Once you finally *feel* the truth of what happened to you and see the depth and breadth of how it continues to affect you, you can heal. You can thrive in the life you were meant to have.

Much of what we'll do together is designed to get at the emotional truth and repercussions of the abuse, feelings that might be buried inside you. But we won't stop there. I'll also show you powerful ways to repair your damaged connection to the self that stumbled into adulthood without a loving guide or a map. In doing that, you'll learn what your parents couldn't teach you: an invaluable set of skills and practices that will give you the resources to live as a healthy, happy adult, using your own buried wisdom to guide you. With courage, determination, and the clear path I'll lay out for you, you can finally release the suffering and burdens of a lifetime.

WHY FOCUS ON THE CHILD?

You may be skeptical about the inner child, which sounds to many people like a meaningless cliché. So I'd like to explain how this work came about, and give you a look at its most powerful elements. Before we get into the work itself, I'll also tell you a bit about the neuroscience that may help explain why it's so effective.

The carefrontation techniques I'll guide you through are the result of more than thirty years of clinical practice with thousands of adults who were abused as children. When I began my career, there was little awareness of the epidemic of abuse perpetrated against children by their caretakers and other people in their lives. The government had scarcely begun tracking child-abuse cases, and there was no public discussion of incest. The adults I saw early on had grown up in a time when children were seen almost as their parents' property, subject to the parents' rages, neglect, or sexual abuse, because what happened behind closed doors was often considered to be "family business," not a matter for outside concern or intervention.

Freud's theory that children went through a phase of fantasizing about sexual contact with their parents—and were therefore to blame for "seducing" them if sexual abuse occurred—was accepted in many circles. One of the textbooks being used by psychology students then speculated that not only was incest extremely rare, but it did no harm. The authors believed it might even be beneficial, because children (never called victims) were "allowed" to act out their fantasies of having sex with a "safe" adult—and both sides might enjoy it.

But the lives of my clients made it very clear that the damage inflicted by every kind of childhood abuse is soul deep, and that it affects every part of life. It also became apparent to me that many of the problems for which my clients sought therapy had their roots in the trauma of being abused as children. I began questioning my clients early and directly about abuse, because frequently, we could trace long-standing problems with relationships, anxiety, self-esteem, depression, panic, self-harm, addictions, and more to physical, sexual, or emotional abuse in their past.

The suffering and despair I saw in people who had endured childhood abuse was intense. In searching for ways to help them, I experimented with techniques that ranged from talking about their pasts to psychodrama exercises in which they acted out scenarios from their lives.

The work that John Bradshaw, the counselor and author, did with the inner child—the part of the self that carries the energy of the children we were—spoke to me. It made intuitive sense that healing the damage of the past had to involve understanding and working with the child who had been abused. My clients' greatest growth, no matter what technique I used, seemed to occur when we came in contact with that child—when we talked *with* the child instead of just talking about it. People got a sense of peace and healing from Bradshaw's technique of imagining the child at various ages and doing short rituals to grieve its losses. But making brief contact with the child didn't seem adequate to me. I began spending more time in focused dialogues with the child, and my clients seemed to benefit most when they stayed in contact with that part of themselves.

The dialogues became particularly revealing when I discovered the work of Lucia Capacchione, an art therapist who, in the 1980s, popularized the concept of writing (or drawing) with the nondominant hand (usually the left) to connect with the right side of the brain, which we thought of then as the "creative" hemisphere.

I asked my clients to try using Capacchione's technique, writing questions for the child with the dominant hand and "letting the child answer" with the nondominant hand. As they did, they seemed to connect to the child in profound and surprising ways. The "voice" of the child that came through in the writing had a quality that felt real to all of us. I'd asked people to write to the child before, but now, when they used the nondominant hand, the child seemed less wordy, more emotional. Often, it was full of fear and anger. The child seemed to view the world as though the abuse was still going on, and it was constantly on guard, sometimes terrified.

The feelings of the child, and its sense that it was always in danger, seemed to be playing out in clients' everyday lives, even though they may have talked at length to other therapists about what had happened to them and understood on a logical level that they were adults now, and safe.

We needed to bring the child into the present. I thought about what part of the self was in the best position to communicate with the child, and reassure it that it was safe, and I began to assign that job to the healthy adult part of the client. No matter how severe the abuse people had suffered, I saw that a part of them was competent. *That* was the part that could listen to the child, learn from the child, and bring the child into the safety of today.

To make the relationship between the healthy adult and the wounded child feel vivid and real, I asked clients to actively imagine they were caring for an actual child and were responsible for keeping it safe and healthy. Though they were sometimes incredulous or extremely skeptical about being able to do that, the healthy adult in them almost always stepped forward to look out for the child.

As that healthy adult took charge of the child's life—which was, in fact, the patient's life—people healed. My clients and I were not researchers testing theories of personality or approaches to trauma, but as we worked to soothe the hurt inner child and empower the adult, we refined a process that finally brought relief from lifelong loneliness, fear, and pain. People transformed suffering they thought they would have to endure forever, and graduated from therapy into happy, healthy lives.

A PROCESS WITH A BEGINNING, MIDDLE, AND *END*

This book is a map that can guide you through the process of healing by learning to rescue, and love, your inner child. It will give you the techniques and exercises my clients have used so successfully, and help you meet the challenges along the path. This is difficult work, and I strongly suggest you do it with the support of a therapist or therapy group that can help you deal safely with the emotions that will arise. Working person-to-person is important for many reasons. The child part of the self receives powerful healing from the presence of a strong, secure adult, whose nonverbal physical cues can give you a comforting sense of safety and acceptance. You didn't get that when you were growing up, and it's something you can't get from a book. I provide that kind of loving presence, along with individual guidance, for my clients, and a therapist can do that for you.

But it's extremely valuable for you to know the techniques I'll describe for working with the inner child moment-by-moment through the day, and you'll also benefit greatly from having a clear vision of how the process of healing can unfold for you. Without a map like this, you can find yourself spending years in a kind of talk therapy that ignores the child and does little or nothing to help you. That's what most of my clients experienced before they came to me.

This process of repairing and reparenting the child part of the self is not meant to last forever. It has a beginning, a middle, and, most important, it has an *end*. At each stage, I'll help you face what happened to you as a child, with deepening care, love, and kindness toward yourself. I've only given the specific label "carefrontation" to the last stage, but everything we'll do is grounded in the larger carefrontation process of learning to care for the child inside you and finding the courage to confront the truths you find. Let the title of this book remind you that care comes first.

The process starts with making a commitment that the healthy adult inside you will reach out to the hurt child and care for it as if it were a "real" child—seeing to it that the child gets adequate food and rest and that it's always protected from danger. You'll begin writing with your "other hand" to communicate with the child, and you'll learn to approach that part of yourself with curiosity, respect, and kindness—things the child was deprived of because of the abuse.

As you establish trust with the child, you'll start to talk to it about the past. You'll let the child teach you about what it's experiencing when something in your life triggers its panic, and you'll help it calm down. I'll teach you techniques you can use to soothe your physical body, which is also actively involved in memories of the abuse. And I'll show you how the child can begin to help you find your way back to pleasure and fun, which I'm guessing have been missing from your life for a long time.

In the middle of the process, the child—and you—will become more able to feel that the abuse really is in the past, and you will know in both your mind and heart that you were not responsible for what happened. I'll help you free yourself from old patterns of victimization and move beyond any lingering sense of waiting for someone else to rescue you from difficulties in your life.

You'll learn skills your parents or caretakers couldn't teach you: how to set boundaries with other people, especially those who were responsible for your abuse. How to say no. How to say "I want"— and most important, how to *know* what you want, and feel entitled to getting it.

As the healthy adult part of you takes charge, I'll help you match your behavior in the world to the feelings that are changing inside you. You'll feel lighter and freer as you step away from hiding and drop the child's old survival tactic of putting other people's needs ahead of your own. You'll learn to step to the center of your own life. Here, I'll also introduce you to an especially helpful part of yourself, your wise essence, which I call the One Who Knows.

Finally, I'll help you take the concrete action that most fully puts your healthy adult self in charge of your life: telling your abuser or abusers how their abuse affected your life, and asking them to take responsibility for the way they harmed you. Doing this demonstrates to the child in the most powerful way possible that the healthy, powerful adult you are now is fully in control. It is that adult who looks the abuser(s) in the eye and holds them accountable. I call that meeting a carefrontation, because it is a necessary confronting that will show you how much you care for the child. It lays the foundation for a relationship with the abuser(s) that is based on truth and honesty rather than secrecy and lies.

The prospect of carefrontation may seem extremely frightening to you right now, but you have not yet become the person whom I will ask to do the carefronting. That person, the one who stands at the end of this process, can look at the abuser(s) through the eyes of an adult not those of a petrified child. That person no longer feels the terror of abuse that happened long ago.

That person is you, healed and whole. Living fully in the richness of the present.

Free.

TRAUMA AND YOUR BRAIN

To heal from trauma, you need to know what happened to you. Usually we think of that in terms of remembering and integrating the story of the abuse, which will be a strong element of this work. But it's also helpful to know what happened on the biochemical level, where the abuse left imprints that have significant effects on the way you experience your life. In the past fifteen years, brain imaging has helped neuroscientists explain some of the mysteries of how abuse affects memory and brain development, so I'd like to give you a brief, simplified picture of the findings I find most intriguing. Trust me when I say there's not going to be a quiz. But if you stick with me, you'll gain a better understanding of why it has been so difficult for you to recover.

We know today that abuse and neglect in childhood change the way the brain develops. The experience of abuse puts the brain's focus on survival, and the parts of the brain that help us navigate threat become more active and fully developed than the parts devoted to reasoning, introspection, and making sense of experience.

The right side of the brain, which specializes in emotion, comes heavily into play in abuse. It registers all the nonverbal cues, emotions, and *sensations* that come with experience—the images, sounds, smells, tastes, touch—all without language or a sense of time. In trauma, parts of the left side of the brain—where words, reason, and analysis reside—often go offline, so memories of the abuse are stored on the speechless right side. And because those memories have not been attached to time or language, two import-ant things can happen.

First, as long as memories are only stored in the right brain, we aren't conscious of them. They're part of our experience, but it's an experience we haven't named or understood. We don't know the memories are there until something triggers them and brings them to the surface. A second quality of these memories is that they are vivid, rich with sensory detail and emotion. And because they haven't been processed by the left brain, which has the job of placing them in time and context, when they surface, it's as though they're hap-pening right now. They don't yet have the left brain's understanding of sequence, or of cause and effect.

You could think of the child part of us that endured the abuse as being stuck there, in the right side of the brain, living and reliv-ing the memories of the abuse. Those memories keep the threat-detecting parts of the brain on alert for anything that could bring another instance of abuse. That can mean they might read any raised voice, any gesture an abuser might have made, or any sensory element of the environment today that resembles the abuse of the past as a potential threat—even a matter of life and death. The threat-detecting system triggers the hormones that make our hearts race and our stomachs clench and prepare us to fight, run, or— when we feel overpowered—simply freeze. But we often have no idea we're reacting to a memory of the past and not the situation in front of us. All we're aware of is a jolt of rage or fear or shame or ter-ror that we interpret as a logical response to what's happening now.

One key part of recovering from the abuse involves turning down the sensitivity of the threat-detection system, so our bodies are not constantly on high alert and our minds can be guided by reason instead of staying in an instinctive survival mode. That allows us to activate the reasoning part of the brain and safely bring the hidden memories into our awareness. As we make conscious connections between the reactions we're having now and what happened during the abuse, we can put the past back in the past and rewire our brains for pleasure, connection, and satisfaction—by giving ourselves the experience of having them.

SOME THEORIES ABOUT WHY INNER-CHILD WORK WORKS

I (and modern neuroscience) learned all this long after I developed my methods of working with the inner child and had already helped generations of clients heal from abuse. I've known what works for them for many years now, and I've been fascinated in recent years to see theories that might explain more about *why* the techniques I'll teach you are so effective.

A school of therapy called Internal Family Systems Therapy, developed in the 1980s and '90s by Richard C. Schwartz, also deals with the relationship between parts of the self, and it too works with the relationship between the healthy adult part of the self and the traumatized child part, while also looking at many other internal parts. People have guessed about what happens as the healthy adult part of the self listens to the inner child. The speculation is that as the adult takes charge of the child, the parts of the brain involved with reason, analysis, and language become activated and the "emotional" parts of the brain, along with the threat-alert system, become quieter.

Another theory, posed by a researcher in London who's applying mathematical models to ideas about how the brain works, is that as the adult self imagines and interacts with the inner child, the brain creates new neural networks that establish the parent-child bond that the child never got from the abusive caretaker(s).

As far as how writing with the nondominant hand works, no one's done a study mapping brain activity as people do this, or connected the scientific dots about what happens in the mind. My guess is that, at the very least, writing with the nondominant hand slows down our ability to use the usual pathways to the language centers of the brain and perhaps makes it easier to access our emotions. It could be too that seeing the shaky, childlike handwriting produced when you write with your other hand makes it easier to imagine and identify with what the child has to say. What I know from what I've seen again and again is that the child and its feelings appear on the page, and its words go straight to the heart.

I promise you, you won't need any kind of theories, or a model of the brain on your desk, to heal. What you *will* need is commitment, an openness to getting to know the hurt child inside you, and a willingness to stand up for that child. As you'll see, this is heart work, designed to bring the child out of hiding and help put the abuse in the past, so it won't keep creating chaos in your everyday life.

The only way to do this is to work at it in a focused, loving way.

HOW TO USE THIS BOOK

As we get started, you'll need to gather some tools: a few childhood photos of yourself from the time the abuse began and when it ended, a pen, a notebook, and a recording device (your smart phone has this capability).

In the notebook, you'll record your progress and document your growing relationship with many parts of yourself. Keep it in a safe, private place.

It's fine to read the chapters that follow all the way through before doing the assignments, but be sure you do more than read. Bring everything you have to the work, even if you feel skeptical.

Because you'll come in contact with buried feelings that may be intense, I urge you to bring this book to a therapist who will read it and support you as you work your way through it. It's important that you find a person who specializes in trauma and abuse, and who has a familiarity with inner-child work. Be sure you feel comfortable with him or her. Don't work with anyone you don't trust, anyone who does not believe you, or anyone who suggests you were in any way responsible for the abuse you suffered.

A therapy group that is willing to work with the book can be another source of comfort, encouragement, and support.

Be gentle with yourself. We'll take things a step at a time.

Let's get started.

1

WHERE DOES IT HURT?
Recognize Childhood
Abuse by the
Scars It Leaves

Bill, an accountant in his mid-thirties, was almost apologetic when he came in for his first appointment. "Look, I'm only here because some friends said you helped them a lot," he told me. "I know you work with people who went through hell as kids, and seeing someone like you might be a little too dramatic for me. I mean, you're about trauma, and I don't know if I qualify. Some stuff went on in my family when I was a kid, and life was crazy. My parents were addicts, and I ended up one for a while, but it's not like they beat the crap out of me or something."

Bill was short and slender, with dark hair, and he had a quick smile that didn't seem to match his sad brown eyes. He had been clean and sober for eight years, he was good at his job, and all things considered, he told me, life was pretty good.

"So what brings you in today, then?" I asked. "Maybe you could tell me something about that stuff that was going on when you were a kid."

"The quick story is this," he said. "Basically, my parents were both seventeen when I was born. They were attractive and wild and they were addicts. Lots of charisma, lots of unmanageable stuff."

His parents, Bill said, fought constantly, and when he was six, his father took off, leaving him alone with his mother, who was alcoholic and depressed. She'd go to bed for days, closing the drapes and keeping the lights off. Just a first-grader, Bill was left to do everything in that dark home—feed himself, get himself to school, beg his mother to eat. He graduated to buying food and counting out his mother's pills, always fending for himself, a "little adult" who had no one to care for him. His mother graduated to heroin.

"By the time I was thirteen, fouteen, I really needed a drink," Bill said. "I began a slow decline into alcoholism, which culminated when I was twenty-three, hospitalized, sexually assaulted, and arrested."

He looked at the wall behind me as the story rushed out. It sounded like he'd told it often, and he even paused for a laugh after "I really needed a drink."

"Fast-forward. I get sober, I'm leading my life, and it starts to get good. Then, when I'm two years sober, my mother ODs and dies. When she's gone, I learn a lot about coping. I stay sober, but I have really faulty coping mechanisms."

I asked what he meant by "faulty coping mechanisms," and Bill told me he'd been picking up men and having sex with them, perpetually on the edge of danger. "On one level I'm this really responsible guy, and I help people and I'm doing okay. But the thing is," he said, finally slowing down, "I feel like shit. I've got the physical sobriety, but I'm in the same kind of pain I had when I was drinking, and I don't know why."

He continued, "I was in a relationship for four years, but we split up a few months ago, and it was my fault. It's always my fault. I don't know why I'm in this situation. I know what to do, I'm doing what I'm supposed to be doing, I'm working the Program. I don't know what's wrong with me."

He sank back in his chair, almost physically deflated.

"I don't think I can blame this all on my childhood," he added. "I'm not sure you're the right kind of therapist for me. I didn't get sexually abused, I didn't get burned with cigarette butts. I just had messed-up addicts for parents."

We sat quietly for a moment.

"Let me ask you a question," I said. "If someone were to burst into this room and stab me seventy-three times and I die, and then they shoot you once in the heart and you die, which is worse? We both die. The effect is the same. I'm not sure it matters what the abuse story is. Whether your parents beat you or just threw you into chaos and let you raise yourself, it hurts you the same way."

"You're gonna have to tell me more about that," he said. "It sounds like it could be true."

Neglect, and every kind of abuse—physical, emotional, sexual—all have the same kind of effects on a child's brain and mind, and leave lasting emotional wounds on the adults they become. The constant anxiety, and even terror, that a six-year-old Bill felt at being left to care for himself and his mother, instead of having the safety and guidance he needed as a small child, wired his brain for fear. So does being told you're stupid and bad, not capable of navigating the world. Or living with people who are supposed to keep you safe but instead beat or rape you.

A child's bond with his or her caregiver(s) teaches the child what to expect of the world. A "good-enough" caregiver, one who pays regular attention to the child, offering comfort and reassurance, creates an enduring sense of security. Children who grow up with that become adults with an inner sense of safety that makes it possible to trust, love, connect with other people, and take the risk of being who they would most like to be.

But when that doesn't happen, when you're in peril at home and the people who are supposed to provide affection and safety instead put you in jeopardy or act as predators, the "survival" part of your brain experiences the world as a dangerous place, keeping you guarded and on alert. The neural connections there are reinforced each time they're activated, and rather than developing the "wiring" for pleasure or play, you become hypersensitive to potential threats in your environment, and you live in fear.

That gives rise to a wide range of symptoms in your life. Addictions of all kinds become common, in part because they calm the physical effects of the body's threat-response system. Relationships are difficult to develop or maintain. A recognizable pattern of suffering—one that's common to everyone who has faced childhood abuse—takes shape.

If you have suspicions that the problems in your life today are connected to what happened to you when you were a kid, you don't have to start by diving into your deepest, darkest memories for evidence. Just as you can track a bear by the shape of its footprints and the fur it leaves on the trees it lumbers past, you can spot abuse by the distinctive marks it leaves on your life.

I want to emphasize that you're not "doomed" or "permanently damaged" because of your early experiences. You can, and will, repair your life with the work we do. But first, let's look at what your life today is telling us about how you were affected by the treatment you endured as a child.

THE TELLTALE SIGNS OF ABUSE

What's going on in your life right now? Are you depressed, not getting what you really want out of life? Do you even know what you want? Do you have a feeling you've sabotaged your career, your relationships, your happiness? Do you tend to feel overwhelmed by even the smallest stresses, and tend to overreact?

The following checklist covers a wide array of the aftereffects of abuse—a collection that includes such disparate-seeming items as low self-esteem, high risk-taking, trust issues (too much or too little), addictions, and always being the "responsible one."

As you go through this list, highlight any items that apply to you. You may not relate to the word "abuse," and if not, just mentally set it aside for the moment and keep marking the items that sound like you.

Abuse Aftereffects Checklist

ISSUES WITH RELATIONSHIPS:

☐ I really want a relationship, but I get scared when people get too close.

☐ I'm lonely a lot.

☐ I've sometimes compromised my integrity and done things I don't want to, to keep someone interested in me.

☐ If I get sick, there's no one to look after me.

☐ People take me for granted.

☐ I don't feel like anyone really knows me.

☐ I have a hard time setting limits and saying no.

ISSUES WITH ANXIETY:

☐ I try not to attract attention. I feel exposed and vulnerable when people notice me.

☐ I feel anxious a lot of the time.

☐ I don't believe happiness can last.

☐ I'm always waiting for the other shoe to drop.

☐ I've never gone for what I really wanted.

☐ I have a sensitive "startle response"—someone's tone of voice or look can make me jump or freeze.

ISSUES WITH CONFIDENCE, SELF-IMAGE, AND SELF-WORTH:

☐ I feel like a fraud.

☐ I look like a competent, functional person on the surface, but I'm falling apart inside.

☐ If people knew what I'm really like, they'd run away.

☐ I feel worthless.

☐ Deep down, I know I'm damaged goods.

☐ I don't know what I want anymore. I focus on other people's needs so much, I lose track of my own.

☐ I either feel like I'm better than everyone else or less than everyone else.

☐ I feel like I'm a bad person with something to hide.

☐ I often feel guilty. I don't really trust myself.

☐ I have a hard time accepting praise or believing I've done a good job.

☐ I believe if I'm not perfect and if I don't do what other people want, I can't have love and respect.

☐ I feel like everybody knows the rules for "normal life" but me.

☐ I just don't seem to fit in anywhere.

ISSUES WITH TRUST:

☐ I'm always the responsible one. It's the only way I know to keep things from falling apart.

☐ I either don't trust anyone or I trust the wrong people.

☐ I don't get my hopes up. People often let me down.

ISSUES WITH POWERLESSNESS:

☐ I feel helpless.

☐ I want someone to save or take care of me.

☐ I always seem to wind up a victim.

☐ I feel overwhelmed a lot.

☐ I wonder if I'll ever have the life I want. I feel like I'm living out what someone else wants.

ISSUES WITH HEALTH AND WELL-BEING:

☐ I've had a lot of digestive problems.

☐ I've had problems with chronic pain.

☐ I work long stretches without eating, taking a break, or going to the bathroom.

☐ I don't feel like I'm fully in my body sometimes.

☐ I take crazy risks (with my safety/health) to feel alive.

☐ I have a lot of issues around sex (don't enjoy it / avoid it / escape into it).

☐ I've had struggles with addiction (alcohol, drugs, food, sex, shopping, Internet, work).

☐ I don't remember what it's like to take a vacation or have fun.

ISSUES WITH EMOTIONS:

☐ My temper can get out of hand.

☐ I feel scared by anger.

☐ I've cut off or confronted other drivers because of road rage.

☐ I struggle with depression.

☐ Sometimes a common experience such as taking a shower or smelling a certain smell triggers a strong feeling of fear in me.

☐ I feel numb.

☐ I can't really talk about or even name my feelings.

☐ I've thought about killing myself so I can have some peace.

How does your list look?

Bill took the list home to think about it and returned the next week saying, "Maybe you should just ask me which ones I *didn't* check."

Many people who haven't labeled their childhood experience as abusive, or who assume their childhood treatment is no longer affecting them, are surprised to find themselves checking off so many items that "the page is one big checkmark" as one of my clients put it.

They're also relieved. Because they see, sometimes for the first time, that the common denominator in the recurring patterns in their lives—the relationships that never really gel, the joy that never comes, the sense of confidence that always eludes them—isn't "I'm screwed up."

It's the abuse. And that's true whether the mistreatment you experienced was physical, sexual or emotional, or involved physical or emotional neglect.

If you're used to taking responsibility and blame for everything that happens, that might sound like an excuse, a rationalization. You may still wonder if what happened to you was really abuse, even when you can see its fingerprints everywhere you look. But ask yourself this question: If you had (or have) kids, would you be willing to leave them at your parents'/abuser(s)' house? It's likely you wouldn't. None of my clients have ever said they would even consider it.

AN EPIDEMIC OF ABUSE: YOU'RE NOT ALONE

Child abuse plays out in secret, often under the façade of "the happy family," and that's one reason so many people feel isolated in their experience. But studies since the 1970s have documented an epidemic. Some of the best information we have about both the scale of the abuse and its aftermath comes from a study that began in the 1990s. Between 1995 and 1997, 17,000 members of Kaiser Permanente in Southern California completed confidential surveys that asked about their current health as well as their childhood experiences. Kaiser and the Centers for Disease Control and Prevention analyzed the data, looking for relationships between what they called "adverse childhood experiences" and health and well-being in later life.

The study asked about abuse and neglect by giving people these definitions:

PHYSICAL ABUSE: "A parent, stepparent, or adult living in your home pushed, grabbed, slapped, threw something at you, or hit you so hard that you had marks or were injured."

SEXUAL ABUSE: "An adult, relative, family friend, or stranger who was at least five years older than you ever touched or fondled your body in a sexual way, made you touch his/her body in a sexual way, attempted to have any type of sexual intercourse with you."

EMOTIONAL ABUSE: "A parent, stepparent, or adult living in your home swore at you, insulted you, put you down, or acted in a way that made you afraid that you might be physically hurt."

The survey's questions on physical neglect asked if "there was someone to take care of you, protect you, and take you to the doctor if you needed it," as well as if "you didn't have enough to eat, your parents were too drunk or too high to take care of you, and you had to wear dirty clothes."

The question on emotional neglect asked if "someone in your family helped you feel important or special, you felt loved, people in your family looked out for each other and felt close to each other, and your family was a source of strength and support." When someone answered no, they were considered to be emotionally neglected.

Abuse, the study found, was staggeringly common:

- 27 percent of the women and 29.9 percent of the men had experienced physical abuse.
- 24.7 percent of the women and 16 percent of the men had experienced sexual abuse.
- 13.1 percent of the women and 7.6 percent of the men had experienced emotional abuse.

Those findings have been repeatedly supported in other surveys and studies. The CDC estimates that a quarter of the children in the US have been abused or neglected during their lives. In 2014, a government report based on reports by child protective services and other experts estimated that 702,000 children faced abuse or neglect between October 2013 and October 2014.

And what we know is that reported and suspected cases of abuse are only the tip of an enormous iceberg. Many abused kids learn to hide their pain, and they fall invisibly through the cracks.

The impact of this abuse epidemic is profound. Abuse and neglect interfere with a child's normal brain development and impair the ability to learn and to develop social and emotional skills.

The Kaiser/CDC study also found:

- People abused in childhood are at higher risk for heart disease, high blood pressure, high cholesterol, lung disease, liver disease, obesity, and cancer.
- They're also more likely to smoke, abuse drugs and alcohol, have psychological disorders, and attempt suicide.

Treating the underlying cause is vital. For that reason, I want to be explicit in describing the spectrum of behavior that constitutes abuse. My clients often try to talk themselves out of labeling what they experienced as abuse or neglect because it wasn't "extreme enough." But as you'll see, abuse comes in many subtle varieties too.

THE FACES OF ABUSE AND NEGLECT

To give you the clearest sense of what abuse and neglect look and feel like, I'll draw from definitions used by the American Humane Association (AHA), one of the first groups in the country to advocate for the protection of children. I've also pulled examples from my practice to help you see the many shapes abuse can take.

PHYSICAL ABUSE

The American Humane Association defines child physical abuse as "non-accidental trauma or physical injury caused by punching, beating, kicking, biting, burning or otherwise harming a child."

A lot of people think, "I never had an arm broken—I couldn't have been physically abused." But let me assure you, bites, burns, bruises, welts, and cuts count as abuse. One of my clients told me how her mother would grab her by the hair and drag her across the room. And physical abuse doesn't have to break the skin. Slapping, pushing, and shaking can terrorize, and seriously injure, a child.

Imagine even a small adult next to a three-year-old. The force of an adult hand alone could cause serious injury. Why does the adult need to pick up a wooden spoon or a belt or a shoe? The terror begins when the child feels the adult's fury and fears what's coming next.

EMOTIONAL ABUSE

The AHA defines child emotional abuse as "a pattern of behavior by parents or caregivers that can seriously interfere with a child's cognitive, emotional, psychological, or social development."

Under the AHA definition, children were emotionally abused if they were consistently:

- IGNORED by their caregivers (for example, not looked at, not called by name, not stimulated, encouraged, nurtured, or protected)
- REJECTED (for example, ridiculed, not touched, not taken care of, not shown affection)
- ISOLATED (cut off from normal relationships with friends, family, and adults)
- EXPLOITED OR CORRUPTED (drawn into illegal acts such as stealing, drug dealing, or prostitution)

- VERBALLY ASSAULTED (put down, shamed, made fun of, threatened)
- TERRORIZED (bullied, raised in a climate of threats and fear)
- NEGLECTED (for example, not given proper education, guidance, or health care)

Emotional abuse warps a child's sense of self and safety. A parent calls a child stupid, a whore, a loser, a piece of shit—myriad names that have nothing to do with love, or what the child is really like. But the child believes what she's told. She loses faith in herself, feels as though she could never do anything right. Or the parent tells the child everything she feels is wrong: "What do you mean you're sad/hungry/scared? You don't feel that way." The child grows up not knowing or trusting her own emotions.

Kids take everything to heart, and these punishing, spirit-crushing experiences pierce them. Children who experience this kind of abuse grow into adults who've never learned what a parent's love should look like, and the world feels like a place where the bottom could drop out at any second. They're out there on their own, fearful, braced for the worst, and suffering greatly.

SEXUAL ABUSE

Sexual abuse is broadly defined in most states as "an act of a person—adult or child—who forces, coerces or threatens a child to have any form of sexual contact or to engage in any type of sexual activity at the perpetrator's direction," the AHA summarizes.

Drawing a child into sexual activity may involve touching, and children who were sexually abused in this way may have been:

- Fondled—stroked erotically on the sexual organs
- Forced to touch an adult's sexual organs

- Penetrated in the vagina or anus by a penis, finger, or other object

But the abuse may not include touching the child at all. Instead, the child may be deliberately exposed to:

- Adults' masturbation
- Sexual intercourse
- Pornography
- Acts of exhibitionism or indecent exposure

A third category the AHA lists is exploitation. A sexually exploited child may be:

- Solicited or engaged in prostitution
- Used in pornography

As well as these overt forms of sexual abuse, I hear of many instances of *covert* sexual abuse, in which adults put their children in an inappropriate sexual role. It happens when a father treats a daughter like his girlfriend, perhaps taking her on business trips or putting her in the role of confidante about his wife's inadequacies. It happens when a mother discusses her sexual problems with a child of eight or twelve. And it happens frequently when parents insist children keep their bedroom doors open when they undress, watch older children bathe, and otherwise violate the child's right to physical privacy because it gives them sexual pleasure or a feeling of power and control.

One of my clients, Sally, a fifty-year-old nurse, told me about instances of emotional abuse in her past, and she mentioned in passing that from the time she was a small child until she went off to college, her stepfather was in the bathroom every time she showered.

"It was probably nothing," Sally said.

"Don't you find it odd that he was conveniently there every time you went in for a shower and your mother never said anything?" I asked.

"Well, she said that he had to get ready for work. That's just the way things were. He never touched me."

"But how did it make you feel?" I asked.

"It was a little weird," she admitted.

"If you had a daughter, would you ever let that happen?"

"Of course not," she said.

No matter how the people who've abused us, or failed to protect us, explain away situations like Sally's, we know when our personal boundaries have been crossed. And once they have, we might as well have been touched. Long after the violation stops, the "yuck"—the psychological discomfort—stays with us and follows us through life.

Another client, Michelle, a thirty-eight-year-old photographer, told me how close she was to her mother, and described the way she and her mom would sleep in the same bed when her mother didn't have a boyfriend there "so neither of us would be lonely."

"She'd want me to stroke her arms and back, which made us both feel close, and, um, she wanted me to touch her breasts, which she said made her feel better," she told me.

In families like Michelle's, the boundaries get extremely fuzzy. Michelle's mom wanted physical comfort and companionship from her daughter that an adult should have been providing, and Michelle knew she was often a surrogate for a boyfriend. But did that "count" as abuse? she asked. Again, the question "Would you want your child to experience that?" is a good barometer. Having her breasts stroked by her daughter made Michelle's mom feel good. As for Michelle, that telltale yuck shows up when she looks back. She wasn't allowed to say, "No, I don't want to do this. It feels bad to me." Sexualized contact was her mother's demand for "love." And Michelle felt she had to comply.

Was that a form of sexual abuse? Yes.

THE ABUSER'S "NORMAL" ISN'T NORMAL AT ALL

The confusing thing about much abusive behavior is that when you grow up with it, you think it's normal.

- Michelle thought there was something wrong with her because she felt uneasy about what her mother wanted from her.
- My client Steven thought it was "normal discipline" to be beaten and to have his mouth washed out with soap.
- My client Mike told people for years he'd "had an affair" with a well-known car dealer in his town who "mentored" him when he was fourteen. He thought that was normal too. And since he'd enjoyed it at the beginning, he believed he'd been in a consensual relationship.
- My client Tim brought me a photo of himself as a little towheaded kid, and he didn't notice until I pointed it out that in the snapshot he had a black eye. "It was part of everyday life," he said. "It was so normal to me I never even saw it."

Most people who grow up with abuse feel crazy and confused. They don't have anyone to validate their feelings, no one to support them in questioning their abuser(s)' "normal." They don't have anyone to tell them the truth.

So let me lay out the truth for you: *None* of the behavior I've described and defined in the preceding sections belonged in your home. *None* of it was normal. *All* of it was self-serving, illegal, and just plain wrong. It was a crime.

Your abuser(s) towered over an innocent child whose life depended on them and who deserved to be protected. Whether they sexually abused you, rubbed up against you, called you names and belittled you, beat you up, or completely ignored you, you were not protected. You were terrorized in your own home, the one place that was supposed to be safe for you.

If there were people who knew about the abuse and didn't stop it, they aided and abetted the crime. In allowing the terror to continue, they terrorized you too.

Even if you were not directly abused but had to witness a sibling or parent being beaten or emotionally assaulted, you lived in an abusive household and suffered from it. You may not have been subjected to it firsthand, but you lived in fear, unable to help your loved ones, and you felt helpless and hopeless. You were terrified and alone, and those feelings followed you into adulthood, just as they follow anyone who was abused.

In a normal, functioning household, parents and caretakers teach you to navigate life yourself. They give you good ground rules, teaching you to listen to your inner self, experience your emotions and not be afraid of them, and soothe and contain yourself. When you get that kind of grounding in how to be an autonomous person, guided from within, you have a good chance of making it in life as an adult.

But in the chaos of abusive families, abusers dictate reality. Their children's independence doesn't serve them, so they don't nurture it. You're left to figure things out on your own, and though you may do an amazing job, chances are you'll always feel as though you don't really know what's normal, or what you're supposed to be doing to be an adequate adult. You're always on the outside, wondering if you're doing it right, and if you ever could.

When your parents don't give you the basic tools for navigating life, you're set up to feel powerless. You spend your life looking for someone to save you, someone who can tell you what to do, a person you can hand your life over to and say, "Fix me." No one has taught you to stand on your own two feet and be whole by yourself.

You're probably unsure of how you feel in many circumstances. In the chaos of abusive families, children are exposed to so much pain, so many lies, and so much confusion that they learn to mute their real feelings. That makes it possible to keep going, but it means you go through life numb. If you push your anger down, you have to keep your happiness turned down too. You may say, "I'll just feel happy and push away all the other feelings." But in doing that, you turn off the whole emotional spectrum, which means you don't ever experience the richness and colors of life, light as well as dark.

You needed a guide and teacher, and you got an abuser. That wasn't normal. It wasn't normal to grow up with the aftereffects of trauma rippling through your life, either.

People who were abused as kids spend their whole lives asking, "What's wrong with me?" The question that will give them the answers they need, though, is "What *happened* to me?"

THE PROBLEM WITH "BUT IT WASN'T THEIR FAULT"

Bill nodded his head as we ran through the definitions of abuse. "I get it," he said. "I get that I missed out on a whole lot of what I needed to get from my parents. And I get that it was not a good thing for a little kid to be around heroin addicts, or trying to take care of them. I get that.

"But I can't really blame them for it. My mother was only twenty when she had me. A twenty-year-old doesn't really know what's right. She was doing the best she could. She was a victim too!"

That's the most common, and most paralyzing, response I hear from people who were abused: "Yes, they hurt me. But it wasn't their fault."

Clients tell me things like:

- "Yes, he beat me up every night, but he was under so much stress at work back then."
- "Listen, I know my mother didn't do anything when my father was coming into my bed when I was twelve, but we

have a good relationship now. I don't want to mess it up by getting into the blame game."
- "He had a rougher childhood than I did. His parents beat the hell out of him. I can't really blame him for doing the same thing to me."

To them, and to you, I say this: Have you beaten a child lately? Have you "punished" a little boy until there were welts all over his tiny body? Have you groped and raped a teenage girl? Have you raged at a small child and told him he's a worthless piece of shit, day after day after day? Have you come home stressed out from work and beaten the hell out of your kids so you'll feel better? Have you looked the other way while you knew your nephew was raping your daughter in the basement?

I know you haven't. There's no gray area in child abuse. There's no debate over whether it's right or wrong. There's no question of who's to blame and who's responsible—it's the abuser and anyone who didn't stop the abuse they knew, or should've known, was going on. Do not let them off the hook.

Here's the thing that has kept you stuck and suffering for so long: If you don't put the responsibility for the abuse where it belongs—on the perpetrators—you will blame yourself and hold the child who suffered responsible. And that's not fair. In very simple terms, the big person was responsible for the little person. Period.

Your healing depends on forgiving the child and holding that small, innocent person—that child part of yourself—blameless. You'll have to get to know who the child is, what he or she really experienced, and how the child sees the world. You have the power, the strength, and the courage to repair what was damaged, and to give the child exactly what he or she has always needed, so the deepest core of you can thrive.

We'll begin to do that in the next chapter.

2

THE HURT KID INSIDE YOU

Abuse in childhood leaves lasting marks on adult life because it happens during the pivotal time when a boy or girl's brain is still developing, and the child is laying the foundation for how he or she understands the world. In an abused child's world, a raised voice may be the signal for a beating to follow. A parent's hug could be a creepy prelude to fondling or sex. Any question or mistake, any spilled glass of milk, can be the occasion for a withering, unrelenting tirade. There's no safe, predictable place in this environment. Home is a minefield, and there's a war going on. Every day the child has to battle to survive, placate predator parents, and prove his or her worth.

Children's brilliant survival mechanisms get them through, but at great cost. On the physical level, their brains don't develop normally, or process memory in an organized way. The input your senses gather during trauma registers in fragments, and the fragments are stored in the right side of the brain, without input from the story-telling, interpretive left brain. They're vivid and real, alive in your body. But essentially, there's no one to tell the little kid inside you that the abuse is over when your terrible childhood ends.

Wary, fearful, and full of well-honed strategies for staying alive, the kid hunkers down inside like a soldier in a cave who never got the message that peace has been declared. So the kid carries into adult life the fears and impressions that registered during the abuse, along with the strategies and understandings he or she honed in the trenches.

The little kid inside you may have learned to survive by manipulating people or hiding or being goody-good so no one would get upset. That was the child's default mode, but now it's *your* default mode.

Abused children don't get the love and attention they need to thrive; they don't hear affirmations such as: "You're loving and lovable—I love you," "Keep trying and you'll succeed," and "Your gifts and dreams are valuable. Follow them. Follow your heart." They don't learn to trust that the world is a safe place for them and for their dreams. What they internalize instead gives them a crazily distorted picture of who they are and what's possible. In words and actions, their abusers let them know: "You're bad." "You're a slut." "I/they only did it because you were looking for it." "You liked it. You're a pervert." "You're stupid and worthless. You'll never amount to anything." "People only love you when you do what they want." "You don't count and your needs don't count." "You ruined my life." "You're nothing." "You never should have been born."

Adding insult to all that devastating injury, people abused as children may never have learned essential life skills that we assume all adults will have. They're cut off from a sense of themselves and their bodies, and it's very difficult for them to pay attention to their own needs and desires. They lack the basics of self-care, such as eating when they're hungry, knowing when they're thirsty, and sleeping when they're tired. They don't know to ask for what they want. They don't know how to manage the give-and-take of a relationship. Intimacy feels scary. Getting off high alert and just relaxing seems impossible.

Is some of this sounding uncomfortably familiar to you?

The imprint of all this early training is so deep you can't change it with New Year's resolutions to "feel better about yourself" or "put your own needs first for a change." You can't change it by talking about how next time, you're going to ask for a raise or tell your boy-friend to think about someone besides himself.

You have to go back to that kid in the cave, announce that the war's over, and then both repair the damage and give the child the good parent he or she never had.

That's why this work focuses on the kid, and why the ongoing work we'll do is all about building a relationship with that forgot-ten, neglected, and traumatized child. Because the adult can't heal until the child is safe in the present.

Getting to know the child—bringing genuine curiosity, respect, and, eventually, love to that part of yourself—is a way of learning to see your experience through adult eyes, and to reflect on what's hap-pening in a new way. As you interact with the child, you'll slowly bridge the gaping divide that currently exists between your feelings and your intellect, between the experiences hidden in the right side of the brain and the understanding that's available on the left side.

The parts of the brain devoted to reflection are the only ones that can bring understanding, order, and peace to the memories of the abuse that are stored wordlessly inside you right now. And the work we'll do with the child is full of simple tools that will give you daily practice in reflecting on what's happening in your life. It won't feel like meditation, and it won't feel like sitting down one more time to rehash your past. Instead, the healthy adult part of you will be staying aware of the child, mindful of what the child is experiencing and always asking why. Day by day, you'll be creating a new life for the child, and as you do that, you'll also build a new life for yourself.

You don't have to think about your brain. Simply think about your inner child as a sacred being who deserves the care he or she never received. Your child can guide you to the self that was lost to the abuse. In taking care of the kid, you are healing your soul. And when you become the good parent your child never had, you can finally grow into the person you were always meant to be.

THE WORK STARTS NOW: CONNECT WITH THE CHILD

Our first step is very concrete, set right here in the present. Today, we're not going back to talk about what happened to the child or imagine what you might have done for him or her had you been the good parent. Instead, starting now, we're going to create the loving, caring environment this child has always needed. Help has arrived—and it's you.

Right now, summon the healthy adult part of yourself. You have a core that was never touched by the abuse. It's the part of you that picked up this book and that knows it's possible to heal. Imagine that healthy part, and let it know you're putting it in charge of working with the child.

Now take out several photos of yourself from the years you were a baby until you were in your teens. Look closely at the ones taken around the time the abuse took place. Can you see differences in the child's eyes, face, and demeanor before and after the abuse? Take as much time as you need to be with this child. Remember, the healthy adult part of you is here for the child. So am I.

From this point forth, you will care for this child. Take a moment to imagine this. The child will be aware of—and affected by—everything you do. Your kid rides with you in the front seat of your car. Will you really flip off someone in traffic? This child sits at the table with you. Will you really drink that much alcohol? This child watches you. Will you really let yourself get that angry? This child depends on you. Will you make someone this important wait another hour for dinner when he or she is hungry?

Make copies of a photo from the time the abuse started in which you can see the child's eyes, and put them where you will see them during the day. Place them on your phone, desk, wallet, purse, mirror, refrigerator, remote control, sun visor in your car, or wherever you choose. Do not abandon the child. Keep him or her with you night and day.

Ask your child what he or she needs. It's okay to speak aloud to the photo, or just to direct your questions mentally to the child. Listening for the child's answers might feel like making up a reply based on what you would want. That's fine. Take him or her for an early morning walk or run if that feels good. Make sure that this child—this young version of yourself—eats properly, sleeps enough, and stays warm, clean, and safe from harm.

YOU MAY NOT FEEL LIKE IT, BUT YOU'RE QUALIFIED

How do you suddenly become a good parent to the hurt and fearful kid inside after a lifetime of ignoring the child, or never fully realizing he or she was there? By ensuring that your child has all the everyday basics of life that he or she could never count on before: rest, attention, nourishment, regular care—things such as clean clothes, medical and dental checkups, and sunscreen—and protection from unhealthy, threatening, or dangerous situations.

Providing these fundamentals is the daily act of respect that love is built on, and that so many of the people I work with never got to experience. You may doubt that you're up to the task, or think you're not qualified to give the kind of love you never got, but the healthy adult part of you knows the kind of loving attention the kid needs, and you have the ability to provide it, just as you would if you suddenly had to care for a friend's child for a few hours.

At intervals during the day, pull out your photo. Is your child hungry? Tired? Scared? Does the child need to take a nap or drink some water? Does he or she need comfort? Music? A hug? You'll know if you tune in, ask, and listen for the answers.

You also know how to protect your kid. Just as you wouldn't let a child you were babysitting run into the street, get into a stranger's car, take a drag off your cigarette, or drink Bloody Marys instead of milk, you won't jeopardize your kid's well-being by exposing him or her to situations you know are unhealthy or hazardous.

Do right by your little kid, starting now. Imagine this child as a very real, very vulnerable being you will take with you through your days and nights as long as we're working together in this book. The child is not an "imaginary friend." The hurt child part of yourself is as real as you are, and neglecting this being is not an option.

As you make choices through the day, think about how they'll affect the child, and think about what the child needs and wants. If you're like the rest of my clients, you'll find you'll have to—and want to—make some adjustments in your life and routines to protect and nurture the child who's there beside you.

IT'S OKAY IF YOU'RE NOT EXCITED ABOUT DOING THIS. DO IT ANYWAY.

Resistance is common when I give these instructions to clients. Steven, a short, slight stockbroker, was skeptical, to put it mildly, when he realized he'd signed up to adopt little Stevie. He barely smiled as we got acquainted, and he sat rigidly across from me for our whole meeting. He had been in therapy for years, he told me, and didn't have tremendously high hopes for another round.

"I've always sort of struggled and felt that there was something wrong with me, but I haven't been able to get at what the issue is," he said. "I had alcohol and substance abuse, but I got sober at thirty, and now I'm fifty-eight, and I think it just might be something genetic."

He'd come to see me on the advice of his sponsor, and it was clear he was there mostly to check one more commitment off his list. "I've always struggled with relationships," he said matter-of-factly. "Friendships, workplace, intimate, romantic—it's all been tough." He was successful in his business life, he said, but except for a couple of close friends, he felt very disconnected from people.

As we talked, he reminded me of one of the Queen's Guards at Buckingham Palace. He didn't smile, just warily observed me as he held himself ramrod straight, locking every emotion in. When I asked him about his experience with abuse, he told me his father had been distant, his mother would often wash his mouth out with soap, and his uncle had sexually molested both his younger brother and him. He'd been abused at school as well, by a female English teacher who lavished welcome praise and attention on him then crossed the line into writing love notes and kissing. He'd been shattered when he had to testify against her in court once her actions came to light. His mother blamed him for the teacher's abuse, and he blamed himself for everything that had happened to him and his brother.

The thought of being shackled to the troublesome younger version of himself who was the bad guy in so many of the stories of his childhood didn't thrill him. Many people think of the child inside as the one who ruined their lives, and don't want anything to do with the little brat. Steven had spent much of his adulthood trying to forget about that kid, and the whole idea of stepping in now to take care of little Stevie "sounds pretty silly," he said. "It's kind of stupid, if you ask me."

"That's okay," I told him. "Do it anyway for the next seven days and see what happens. You've tried everything else. I promise this will change you. What have you got to lose?"

Steven stared at me. "All right," he said. "All right."

It was the beginning of a relationship that became the most important part of his life.

Trust issues are common at the beginning. Like Steven, many people don't see where this caretaking idea is going, so they balk at the process. They don't trust themselves to follow through, and they don't trust this intruder of a kid who's suddenly going to take up so much space in their lives. Clients often tell me they don't want this child, and they resent the idea that they have to be the one who takes care of the kid. "Why do I have to be the one to work on this shit?" they complain. "It's not fair! I don't want to do this!"

But each time you pause to consider the child's needs, ask how the child is feeling, and find out what he or she wants, you're creating a moment of safety for a part of yourself that has had very little. You may think it's only "imaginary," but your kindness and the concrete actions you take are teaching the child, and maybe even the threat-detecting parts of your brain, that it's okay to relax, to override the wired-in fear.

When you were growing up, you never had someone in your life who was there for you—someone kind, constant, and consistent. But you can be that person for this child. I know that about you. Because you would never treat a child, your child, the way the adults in your past treated you.

BEING THERE FOR A KID WITHOUT A COMPASS

Reparenting that child is the necessary groundwork for everything else we'll do, no matter how "mild" you think your caretakers' treatment of you was. The aftereffects, as we've seen, are the same. Every kind of abuse creates low self-esteem. If there has been emotional abuse, there may be sexual problems too, because it creates such a fear of intimacy. And when there's been neglect—which happens on the emotional as well as the physical level—there's always a feeling of low self-confidence, because a child who's had no one teaching, guiding, setting boundaries, and being there for it is never quite sure if it's "doing it right," the "it" being life.

Amanda, a tall, reserved, thirty-six-year-old mother of two, didn't like putting the label "abuse" on the way she'd been raised. She came to see me because she'd moved to a new neighborhood and had to choose a new kindergarten for her son. "That doesn't sound like it would be a big deal, right?" she asked. "You don't see other moms melting down because of the pressure of getting their kid into the exact right class." But Amanda had worked herself into a tearful, paralyzed state, and her therapist, who thought that might have something to do with the way her parents had treated her when she was little, introduced her to me.

"I think this is just a midlife crisis," Amanda told me. "I know you specialize in trauma and abuse, but I don't have anything in my past you could call that. I grew up in a nice, middle-class home with nice clothes, and no one beat me up or sexually abused me. I'm not in that category, and I've never thought I was." Yet when we looked at the abuse checklist, she was surprised to see she resonated with two-thirds of the entries, especially loneliness and the feeling that she'd missed some important lesson about how to live that everyone else had gotten.

Her father, she told me, was a very religious man who emphasized that there was one right way to do everything—his way, which he interpreted as God's way. To disagree, or make a choice that didn't align with his, was to defy him—and Him. Her mother, who was cold and detached, never had a say, and only deferred to her husband. Amanda was on her own when it came to learning about dating and boys and sex—or any of the many things her parents didn't think it was appropriate to talk about. She was supposed to "do what God wants you to do," she said, "but I didn't know what God wanted, and I seemed to always get it wrong. I argued with my father a lot, but I was always wrong, and he was always right."

Children who grow up in this kind of rigid family regard every choice they make as a matter of life and death. Unlike most other kids, they don't get to make casual, day-to-day decisions between green beans and French fries or short skirts and long ones or accounting class versus hip-hop dance. Their parents impose their own preferences as the only reasonable (and sometimes moral) option.

"That's a pretty lonely place to be," I said, "when your parents aren't there to guide you and give you the tools to go out and make your own mistakes." When caretakers only seem to love you if you manage to think exactly like they do, it seems like the end of the world when you don't do everything right the first time—because the stakes are so high. If you know your own mind and heart and let them lead you, you risk losing the love of the people who control your well-being. But it never feels right to abandon your true desires, either. You're stuck. Indecisive. Frozen. Often people don't think about this kind of control and undermining of a child's self-confidence as abuse, but it is—and it makes it extremely hard to navigate life as an adult. The child is set loose with no map, no compass, and no belief in him- or herself.

"I think we need to go back and get the little girl inside you who feels so confused and scared and sure she's always going to screw up," I told Amanda.

"That feels good to me," she said. "I'm not sure I'll do it right— I've got two flesh-and- blood kids who I don't always know how to take care of—but I will try to help this little girl."

"When you don't know what to do, what she wants or needs, look her in the eye and ask," I said. "You will know."

As well as taking care of her younger self all week, I asked Amanda to do one other thing: While looking at photos of herself as a child, I wanted her to touch base with the sense of loneliness that loomed so large inside her. It seemed to be coming from deep in the past. "Try to remember the first time you felt that way," I said. "It will help you begin to put together the way things were when you were little."

That's something I recommend when you're not sure about when the abuse started. It's a great way to connect with the child and begin to comfort him or her.

Remember that if at any time in this process you begin to feel overwhelmed with feelings from the past, you can walk away from them. Bring yourself into the present by feeling your feet on the floor and the breath moving in and out of your body. Use all your senses: What do you see around you? Smell? Hear? Call a friend, take a walk or run, pet your cat. And if you need to, call your therapist or sponsor. The best thing you can do for your child is to take care of yourself. (You'll find many self-soothing strategies in chapter 5.)

YOU DON'T HAVE TO BE PERFECT, YOU JUST HAVE TO BE THERE FOR THE CHILD

Please don't feel any pressure to be perfect as you take on this task. This work is not about being perfect or acting perfectly or striving toward someone else's standard of perfection. This is about taking small, daily actions for the child's benefit, and doing a little bit of hard work every day: the work of paying attention, thinking about the child, and following through when you know what the child needs and what you'll need to do to provide it. All it takes is a small spark of hope inside to propel this new way of being, which I promise will change your life. It's hope that allows you to say, "Yes, I'll try this, even though I'm not sure I even *have* an inner child." And it's hope that connects you with the scared, dubious child who so wants and needs a parent's love—*your* love.

No one was there for the child to ask, "Is there something wrong? What's going on? Are you okay?" But you're here now. And the healthy adult part of you has the power to help, and heal, that child.

THIS WILL TAKE A SERIOUS COMMITMENT

One thing I will emphasize again and again is that you are not responsible for your hurt, but you are responsible for your healing. If you were in a car hit by a drunk driver, and the collision was entirely that driver's fault, you would still need to commit to participating in your own healing process. You would go to physical therapy and do the exercises you needed to, to recover and grow stronger. In the same way, your abuse was not your fault—you were a victim. But your emotional body was hurt, and you need to heal it. And it's your responsibility to take control of the healing process.

To do that, you'll need to be there for yourself, and for your child, as no one else has ever been. The most effective way I've found to begin doing that is to make a formal commitment to giving the child what he or she has always wanted and needed.

I asked Steven, the stockbroker, to call to mind his young self, and ask himself these questions:

- What do you wish your parents had done for you when you were growing up?
- How would you have liked them to have treated you?
- What did you need from them that you didn't get?
- What kind of actions did you want your parents to take on your behalf?

People often give me answers like: "I wish they had asked me questions to see what was going on." "I wish they had believed me." "I wish they had protected me."

Steven thought a while and said, "I mostly wanted them to be there for me, no matter what I was feeling, and for someone to protect me and my brother, to actually notice we weren't okay, and be awake enough to know that bad stuff was happening in our own house."

I asked him to write a letter to the child inside, making a commitment to address those concerns.

STEVEN'S COMMITMENT LETTER TO HIS CHILD

Here's the letter Steven wrote and brought into our second session:

Dear Stevie:

Please do not worry. I am getting the help you need. I will give you the love and comfort you crave. I will protect you. You will no longer have to be in fear all the time.

You have my promise. I will show up for you. I will walk with you down those dark alleyways to find our soul and heal together. I will listen to your angry words. I will embrace you when your fists want to pound. I will listen to your feelings, and I will not laugh at you, make fun of you, beat you or yell at you. I will compliment your achievements. I will listen to your truths, and I will believe the secrets you hold on to.

I will always believe in you.

I love you.

Steven (Dad)

ASSIGNMENT 1: A Letter, and a Promise, to Your Child

Answer the four questions you saw Steven answer. Then, with the photo of your child in front of you, ask the healthy adult part of yourself to write a letter to that little boy or girl and make a commitment to care for him or her.

You might write something like: "I commit to be there for you, to love you unconditionally, to listen to everything you have to say, and to believe you. I promise to respect you and to protect you and not to minimize your experience."

Keep in mind that this is a personal letter from you to the child, so say the words you know your child longs to hear. Promise you will provide exactly the treatment you hoped to receive from your parents, and consistently give this child the good parenting he or she has always deserved. This commitment letter does not need to be any specific length. Write simply. Write honestly. Write directly, from the heart. Use words the child will understand, and don't worry about being literary or impressing anyone. This is just for the child, and just for you. The feeling you put into it, and your intent to carry through on this vital promise, are all that matter.

ASSIGNMENT 2: Read the Letter and Reflect

Read the letter aloud, and record yourself reading it. Write about what comes up for you when you play back the recording.

YOU WILL EARN THE TRUST OF YOUR CHILD, AND YOUR OWN DOUBTING SELF

Starting out, you may not know exactly what to do or say, or how to think about your kid. But with the photos of your child all around you, make an effort every day to remember your commitment. If you want to reread your commitment letter every morning or evening, do that. If you want to set an alarm on your phone to be sure your child has regular mealtimes and a decent bedtime, do it. The more you show up for the kid, every day, in dozens of small ways, the more you'll trust your ability to do it, and more important, the more your child will trust you.

I learned this early in my career, when I worked at a women's shelter and saw not only women who had been battered but their children, who had grown up scared in an atmosphere of abuse. I thought they'd come running when I offered to listen to their stories about what had happened to them and told them I could help. But that's not the way it worked. They didn't want anything to do with me at first, and I had to prove to them I was someone who cared, by coming back again and again and doing what I said I would.

I know you may have been waiting a long time, maybe a lifetime, to have someone in your life who puts you first and has your best interests at heart, someone who can read your needs and meet them, someone who can listen to your doubts and fears and anger and comfort you, accept you, love you. *You can be that person for your child.* Please take a long look at the beautiful, vulnerable child you were and say: "I'm here. I love you. I won't ever abandon you again."

ASSIGNMENT 3: Mark This Moment With a Photo

Today, take a photo of yourself and keep it in a safe place. This photo, ordinary as it is, will be an important record of where you started, and though you may think this is an unremarkable moment, it's actually a milestone, one you'll want to see clearly when you look back. Put the photo away and don't look at it until we reach the end of our work together. When we take a photo then, you'll be able to see—especially in your eyes—the distance you've traveled, and the wounds you've healed.

3

BASIC TOOLS

In the early days and weeks, connecting with your child is an experiment, and you'll be working out what this relationship looks like. You learn about the child by repeatedly asking "How are you doing? What do you need?" and letting the answer push you to take a caring or protective action.

None of this may feel especially natural or instinctive at first. One of my clients, a legal secretary named Terry who grew up with both physical and sexual abuse, was flustered after a week of carrying a photo of her kid and working hard to suss out the child's needs. "Honestly, it freaked me out to do this," she told me. "My child wasn't saying much, and I didn't know what to say back. Then I realized that the last thing I wanted to do was hear from my inner child. If I give her a voice, I'm afraid I'll never be able to shut her up. I just feel clueless about how to do this. I don't know how to communicate with a grown-up, much less a kid."

These are common fears and realizations, and important ones to keep facing down whenever they arise—especially any thought that tells you, "I don't want to deal with/hear from my inner child."

"I wonder what you're afraid of," I said to Terry. "I wonder what you're afraid the child will tell you as she starts to open up. To re-cover from abuse, you have to look at the heart of the matter, which means listening to what the child has to say. If she's telling you she's uncomfortable or angry or hungry or hurting, you're the one who can hear her. No one before has wanted to hear what she's been through and what she needs. It's up to you to be the one who doesn't let her down."

I told her, "You may not know what to do or say, but keep show-ing up. No parent is perfect, and you won't be, either. It's okay. Be there anyway."

I sometimes hear people saying, "My child is such a pain." But the truth is, until you care for him or her, your child is *in* pain, and you're experiencing the effects in your life every day. The child in-side you, who will start to ask for your attention and let you know how much he or she needs your love, holds the key to your pain, and also to your recovery. As the healthy adult part of you begins to draw the child out, it will become easier to see that the injured child is not the whole of you, and it will become easier for you to examine his or her feelings without becoming overwhelmed.

Getting to the root of your pain by finding out what the child is experiencing takes courage. But as Joseph Campbell said, the cave you fear the most is the cave that holds the treasure. You've got to be brave enough to listen to the kid, and be willing to hear him or her instead of running away. You're the only one left. *It's you or nobody.*

In getting to know your child, and giving that tender being what he or she needs, you have a second chance to take care of yourself, and do it right. You have a second chance at life. Please take it.

I know it will take time for the child to become real to you. But the tools in this chapter will help you see the child more clearly, hear his or her voice, and come to *feel* the child's presence, not just think about it. You'll also feel the presence of the healthy adult part of yourself expanding as you step in to give the child attention or comfort. That relationship will set you both free.

THE ESSENTIAL TOOL: WRITING WITH YOUR NONDOMINANT HAND

One way to ease into the realm of feelings is by exchanging hand-written notes with your child. That sounds like something from an etiquette book, but it's actually a way of imagining the child more fully and giving yourself time to experience what's happening in your physical body and your emotions as you make contact with this part of yourself.

You do it like this: With your dominant hand, the one you automatically use for eating or throwing a ball, write down a question you'd like to ask your child. At first, you'll be asking the child the same sorts of questions you've been asking him or her mentally: "How are you feeling?" "What can I do for you?" "What would make you happy right now?" Then, using your nondominant hand, you let the child answer.

Try it now.

Write this question for your child: "Do you need anything from me?" And then call the image of your child to mind, or look at his or her photo, and move your pen to your other hand. Listen for what the child tells you, and let your nondominant hand write.

My clients call this switching technique "right hand/left hand," because most of them—and most people—are right-handed (though this process is just as valuable for lefties).

People often resist engaging with right hand/left hand at first, because everything about writing with the nondominant hand feels awkward. They also may think they know what they are going to say. But the interesting thing is they don't, because the process interrupts your normal way of thinking and gives you access to a different kind of information.

A DOOR INTO THE "BASEMENT"

Your dominant hand is wired to the language center in the "let's reason it out" portion of the brain, and the writing you do with it reflects what's coming from your analytical mind. But when you write with your nondominant hand, you derail the usual automatic process that connects you with your habitual thoughts.

No one has studied exactly what happens in the brain as you do this, but my guess is that as you imagine the child, struggle to shape letters, and stop to listen for what the child is saying, you use a part of the brain that's activated by imagination and reflection. The medial prefrontal cortex, as it's called, is the center of a system in the brain that creates a sense of who you are moment by moment by moment.

This imagining, reflective part of the brain is able to connect with the emotions and impressions associated with the abuse, which have been hidden in the right hemisphere of the brain. It has the power to override the sensitive threat-sensing systems, allowing unconscious feelings and impressions to be interpreted, understood, and healed.

I like to say that as people write with the nondominant hand, they reach into the hidden repository where the kid has been living all these years, surrounded by all the feelings and sensory memories stored there. As Freud knew, and modern neuroscientists have explained, these unconscious feelings and memories have great influence over our behavior—but they affect us without our awareness. The unconscious mind signals its perceptions, fears, and suspicions with impulses that we react to.

Have you ever noticed yourself responding to something like a kid instead of an adult? Maybe you're hypersensitive to raised voices and automatically get defensive or shrink away, even when it's only your boss being emphatic or someone nearby letting off some steam or enthusiasm. There's no reason to be afraid or take the volume as a threat, yet in your gut you do. You know you're not responding rationally, and it doesn't make sense. That's the inner child running the show from the bunker.

When you grow up with the trauma of abuse, the rational left brain says, "I'm getting the hell away from home and leaving all that behind." But you can't outrun the trauma because it's so vividly registered in the subconscious reservoirs of feeling in your brain. With left hand/right hand, though, you can pull the child out.

CONNECTING WITH THE HEART, AND THE VOICE, OF THE CHILD

Your nondominant hand speaks for the child in the photo you keep with you. Look at your child's photo now. Look at the child's face. Look into the child's eyes, and remember all the secrets you had to keep, all the hurt you held in. Remember all the times you wanted to scream to someone about what was happening to you but couldn't. Remember the times you wished somebody could just look at you and understand you needed help. Remember all the times you wanted to run away or even die.

This child has a lot to say, and you can do more than simply listen. You can embrace the child and tell him or her: "I am here for you, I hear you, I see you, and I will respond." It may seem that you are just wrestling with the pen or making up words, but even in the attempts that feel the most awkward, you are finally giving the child a sense of safety and connection. You are saving this child's life.

ASSIGNMENT 1: Ask Your Child Questions

Take some time now to ask your child questions, using your dominant hand. Let your nondominant hand answer.

You may find it difficult to write with your nondominant hand. Don't worry. Don't judge the quality of your handwriting. Just write. The most important thing is to allow your nondominant hand to tap into what is beyond your conscious mind and let the child's voice come out in your writing. You can use these questions to get you started.

- How do you feel today?
- Is there anything special you want to tell me?
- How can I help you?
- What can I do to make you feel safe?

Whatever the child says or doesn't say right now, he or she is aware of—and comforted by—the way you are reaching out.

THIS CAN BE A CONVERSATION

Jennifer, a forty-one-year-old executive assistant with a halo of curly blond hair, stumbled through her first right hand/left hand attempts. "It's a weird thing to do—I've never done anything like this before," she told me. "I've been trying, but to be honest, sometimes I think this is fucking insane. 'My little child?' In some moments it seems totally crazy. But I promised to do the homework, so I kept sitting down to write to my little girl, and I kept having the feeling, 'I don't want to do it.'

"So I finally thought, 'Okay, what's the big deal?' With my right hand I decided to ask my little girl, 'Why don't you want to do this?' And she wrote back one word: 'Scared.'"

"She probably *is* scared," I said. "What did you tell her?"

"I didn't really do anything," Jennifer said. "That's all she said—nothing else came. So I wrote, 'Why don't you want to talk?' And she didn't say anything else. I tried one more time with that, and that was it. To tell you the truth I was pretty surprised that anything happened at all. But I got what was going on, and that's what's supposed to happen, right?"

"It's a great start," I told her, "but you can do a lot for her. Ask why she's scared. Ask her what would make her feel better. Let her know you're a big person who can protect her."

Jennifer was silent for a moment then burst into tears. "Oh, God," she said. "I just walked away. I abandoned her just like everybody else. It didn't even occur to me to draw her out. This is all so bizarre, I didn't know what to do."

I reassured Jennifer that at first, no one knows what to do. The people in my group sessions call them "parenting class," because that's what we're learning to do. No one taught you what good parenting looks like, so compassionate actions that look "obvious" in retrospect aren't obvious at all.

"Think of the kinds of things you'd like to hear if you were small and scared," I told Jennifer. "That's the best place to start."

"You mean things like 'It's okay. I'm here,'" she said, still crying. "This is stupid, but it really gets to me, thinking about this. I really wanted to hear anyone say that to me."

"That's what you can give this little girl," I said. "All those loving words you wanted so much."

WORDS THAT HELP

Because you probably didn't get much comfort and encouragement as a child, I'd like to suggest some words that will help you soothe and get to know the kid inside. You probably remember what it was like to be lectured by a know-it-all adult who didn't listen, or to be ignored by someone who never picked up on what was going on with you. As a good parent, you'll want to ask questions, keep up your end of the conversation, create openings, and be reassuring. Words like this will help you do that:

- How are you feeling?

- I'm here for you.
- What do you feel like doing?
- You sound sad/scared/angry. What's going on?
- I know it's scary, sweetie. What happened to make you upset?
- What else do you want to tell me?
- I'll keep you safe. I'm not going anywhere.
- I won't let anyone hurt you.
- Let's sit together a while. If you feel like talking, great. And if you don't, we'll just be together. I love looking at your face and thinking about you.
- I'm glad you're here, and we're together.
- What sounds like fun today?
- What can we do to make it better?
- You're so handsome/beautiful.
- I'm proud of you, honey.
- I'm your mom/dad, and I'll always take care of you.
- It's okay. I'm with you now.
- I love you, sweetheart.

EVERY CHILD IS DIFFERENT

Your kid may be so happy to see you that he or she runs straight into your arms and talks up a storm as soon as you start doing right hand/left hand. But he or she may hang back, longing for your interest and protection but afraid. Afraid something bad will happen. Afraid of getting attached to you then being abandoned again.

You may have to go sit down beside your child as he or she eyes you with suspicion. You have to return day after day with kind words and invitations and the support of your presence, your interest, your questions—even when there is no response, or just a word or two. You have to be the person who sees the child waiting for you to prove you'll show up, and surprises him or her by doing it. And you have to keep taking care of the child, doing what you know is best, even if you get little or no response for a long time. I promise you this: Your child will open up and come to you. It may take weeks or even months, but the child will come.

An imagination exercise can help you figure out where your child is, physically and emotionally, which will make it easier to meet the child on his or her own ground.

WORKING WITH IMAGINATION EXERCISES

This exercise will take you into your past. To keep you safe, I'd like you to do a few things before you start:

- Read through the exercise. If walking into the past this way feels scary to you, you don't need to do it. You'll benefit just from reading about other people's experiences. Your child will reveal what you most need to know in right-hand/left hand work even if you skip the exercise.
- If you want to try, and you're working with a therapist, take the exercise into a session and ask to do it there, with support.
- If you are alone, call a friend who knows you and believes you, and let him or her know what you're doing. Arrange to talk right after, just to bring you fully back from your imagination. Set a timer for five minutes before you start to mark the end of the exercise, to prompt you to bring it to a close.

IMAGINATION EXERCISE: THE INVITATION

Sit in a comfortable place where you won't be interrupted, and look at your photo of your child. Breathe deeply and slowly, and when you're ready, close your eyes and pretend you are falling backward through time. Fall backward to the time of the photo. You're safe—

you'll be fine. When you're there, look around. Where are you? Do you see your child? When the child appears, approach him or her. Take the child's hand and go to the place you lived when you were the age of the child in the photo. Where are you?

I want you to take the hand of that little boy or girl and kneel down and tell the child all the things you would've wanted to hear at that age. That you love the child, that he or she is a wonderful person, that you are there to keep the child safe and happy.

Now ask the child if he or she will come with you and let you be the parent. If your child says yes, take the child's hand and lead him or her away from the past and into the place you live now. If the child says no, or doesn't respond, say you are there and will always be there, and you will keep loving and waiting and asking until he or she is ready to come with you. The invitation is forever, and so is your love.

Breathe deeply, with the child's face in mind, and open your eyes.

Brad, a fifty-year-old preacher's son who had grown up with his father's rage, shaming, and abuse, walked into the exercise with no expectations.

"My brain was saying 'This will never work,' but all of a sudden I was in the courtyard of the house I grew up in, and I could see myself as a little boy," he said. "I went to him and put my arm around him and told him he didn't have to be so scared. I told him that I loved him and he was so handsome and good-looking. And when I asked him to come with me he just lit up. He said yes, just like that. I could tell he was surprised. I was surprised too. And I led him away from that terrible house. It broke my heart open to be able to do that."

Don't worry if your child is not ready to walk with you right now. You're opening to the child no matter what happens. The invitation you made *was* registered, and it meant everything to the child inside you.

CHILDREN IN HIDING

If you're having trouble connecting with your child, you may want to use a variation of the imagination exercise as a brief guided meditation to help you visualize the child in a particular location: his or her hiding place.

Steven, the stockbroker who'd faced sexual abuse from his uncle and teacher, felt frustrated and defeated when his first attempts at right hand/left hand were met largely with silence. "I must be doing something wrong," he said. "I'm not getting anything."

To help Steven sense and imagine the child more clearly, I asked him to do just the first part of the "Invitation" exercise. He relaxed in his chair, back straight and feet flat on the floor, and centered himself with deep breaths, concentrating on long, slow exhales.

"Close your eyes and fall back in time until you're in the time where your kid lives," I told him. "Where are you when you look around? Where do you feel your kid is stuck or hiding?"

"He's under the bed!" Steven said after a long while. "That's where I used to go after being abused. He's making himself as small and invisible as he can, and he's not coming out."

Steven was quietly desperate to recover and feel better, so he'd been faithfully checking in with little Stevie about what he needed, and, though he was receiving no answer, he was doing his best to care for him. But it was like trying to have a relationship with a rock.

"My child doesn't want to talk to me at all," Steven told me when he came out of the exercise. "My child does not trust anybody, doesn't trust me. I know what it feels like under the bed, and that's where my boy is emotionally. As far as he's concerned, it's, 'No, I'm not talking to anybody.' I'll be lucky to get him to say one word. What do I do with that? He doesn't want to talk."

"Just be a loving parent, very gentle," I told him. "He's scared. Don't force him to say anything. You can just say, 'Okay, if you feel like talking later, let me know.' It takes patience and practice, but keep at it. You know how when someone is in a coma, the family keeps going to the bedside and talking to them? We know that even when people don't respond, they're taking in every word. And we know it because when they do wake up, they remember, and they tell us those words brought them back.

"It's similar with your child. Now you know he's under the bed and not inclined to come to you. But he can hear you, even if he won't speak to you yet. He can hear every word, and feel every-thing you do for him. And that's what will bring him out and give him relief."

"The kid is just so afraid," Steven said.

"Stay with him," I said. "That's what he needs the most."

DAILY PRACTICE 1: GOOD NIGHT AND GOOD MORNING, AN EVERYDAY CHECK-IN

Routine will help you keep your child in mind, so now I'd like you to use right-hand/left-hand writing to make contact with your child at the end and beginning of every day.

Good Night

This evening, before you go to bed, write with your domi-nant hand and ask your child these questions.

- Is there anything you want to tell me?
- What do you need from me?
- How was your day?

Answer each question with your nondominant hand. Then, with your dominant hand, write a response. Ask questions, and close by saying "Good night" and letting the child know he or she is safe with you.

Good Morning

In the morning, check in with your child again. With your dominant hand, write:

- How are you feeling this morning?

Let the child answer through your nondominant hand. Then, with your dominant hand, write a reply. Reassure him or her, and sign off by saying "Have a good day!"

IF YOU HAVE DOUBTS

Many of the people I work with have been through so much therapy, with so much dashed hope, they're tentative about using right hand/left hand. My client Lisa, a fast-talking thirty-two-year-old event planner, had been molested by her father and brother through her childhood and fought suicidal thoughts all her adult life. She walked in saying, "I'm incapable of intimacy and I can't be fixed." Lisa froze at the thought of writing to her child. She said, "In rehab, my therapist had an empty chair I was supposed to talk to. That did nothing. And this dorky writing is supposed to? Listen, I was never a kid, I'm never gonna be a kid, and that's it. I don't get what good this is going to do."

I told her what I'll tell you: Your best thinking did not solve the problem of your past, or help you find the sense of peace and connection with other people that you want so much. But having these odd little written conversations will begin to take you out of your head and into your heart and soul. Perhaps you feel as though you never had a chance to be a child. But the small, vulnerable person in the photo clearly was one. Write to *that* child with curiosity about who he or she is and what he or she is experiencing. Set the intention that you'll create an atmosphere of safety around the child in all you say and do.

Don't overthink this stuff. If you really want to think about it, do it *after* you do your right-hand/left-hand writing to the child, and *after* you offer the child the best care you can. You know how it works in theory. Now you can find out how it works in practice.

You don't have to set aside hours and hours of your day for this. Just take that first small step.

Everyone you'll meet in the book started out just where you are now, hopeful and scared and doubting and wanting to believe. And all of them persisted and healed. You can do this too.

4

TELLING YOUR STORY

The story of your abuse has shaped you, and the understandings that flow from it—about who you are, what's possible for you, and what you can expect from other people—color every minute of your life. What happened in the past seems unchangeable. It happened. It's over. But it lives inside you, and it's extremely valuable to pull it into the light and see how it is affecting what's going on in your life.

You may think you've told your story a million times and that rehashing it one more time won't make any difference. Or you may have big gaps in your memory and a hazy feeling about what might have happened. Wherever you are, whatever you remember, what I want you to focus on now is telling your story as plainly and completely as you can.

We'll use your story as both a diagnostic tool and a healing one. Our goal is to slowly integrate your adult memories of the abuse with the emotions that have been locked away with the wounded child inside. The story you write will show you what your mind knows, acknowledges, and believes today about what happened.

Because the trauma of abuse creates such powerful feelings of rage, sadness, fear, and abandonment—most of them stored outside of our awareness—it's common to feel numb or intellectualize and look on your story from a great emotional distance. While memory that's processed through both sides of the brain is constantly shifting, picking up new meanings with time, abuse memories are frozen in a space that feels timeless and never-ending. The work we'll do will help change that, and we'll return to the story along the way to see how it changes, how your understanding evolves.

I talk with clients about how they need to own their own story, instead of letting it own them. By that I mean that as you heal, you'll be able to talk about what you experienced without feeling overwhelmed by the emotions of the past, including rage at the abuser(s), and you'll develop great sympathy for the child who suffered so much. We'll unwind your story from the stories your abuser(s) have told and the harsh judgments you may have internalized about somehow having "deserved" the abuse or "overreacted" to the harm you faced.

Our first task is to get the facts as you understand them now out of your head and onto paper. It's not important to create the "etched in stone" version that must stand for all time. You'll write your story more than once in the course of this work, and revise it as your understanding deepens. The next versions may include incidents that you'll remember much later, or feelings that surface along the way, so let's think of this as the first layer of the story—what your conscious mind knows today.

BEGIN WRITING YOUR STORY

It may seem abrupt to jump into this writing so early in the process, but because your story is our starting point, and our focus, I consider it to be an essential first step. Between the time I see clients for the first time and their next session, usually one week later, I ask each of them to put their story on paper. This, along with our work with the child—who will need special care, comfort, and attention during this time—will take us to the heart of this healing work. I'd like you to read through this entire chapter first, and then go back to write what you remember. You can do this. Just take it one step at a time.

PREPARATION

Find a quiet place where you won't be disturbed, and set aside twenty to thirty minutes for thinking and writing. This work will probably take you several hours in all, but it's fine to take it slowly, in twenty- or thirty-minute bites. You can make good progress, and minimize your chances of becoming overwhelmed, by allowing yourself to write in one short stretch each day until you've finished. It's fine with me if you want to take this even more slowly. If you need to take a long break after writing for the first time, you can commit to writing twenty minutes once a week until you've completed your story. Just be sure to make a firm appointment with yourself to complete each installment, and keep it. Don't wait until you're "in the mood" or "inspired" to write. Book the time and be faithful to this work.

The abuse has made you ultrasensitive to threats in your environment, and it will be difficult for you to write if your body feels alarmed by the prospect of looking at your memories of such a painful time in your life. So if you feel any anxiety before you start to write, calm yourself with slow, easy breaths, making your exhales longer than your inhales. Feel the heaviness of your feet resting on the floor and the weight of your hands. You're safe. It's okay to remember.

COMMUNICATE WITH YOUR CHILD AND BEGIN TO REMEMBER

Pull out your photo or photos of your kid and take a good, long look at the child you were at the time you were being abused. Write a note to that child with your dominant hand, saying "I love you" and letting your little boy or girl know you will be remembering some scary things but you're here to protect him or her, that it's safe now. Reassure the child that everything you'll be writing about is in the past. Ask how the child is feeling, and with your nondominant hand, let the child reply. If the child needs reassurance, offer comfort. It can feel especially soothing to stroke your arm gently as you tell the child, "It's all right. You're safe with me. I'll take care of you."

If your child is agitated or upset about the prospect of you reentering the past in your imagination and memory, or if you are worried about doing so, be sure to seek support. You may want to do this writing in the company of your support group, therapist, or a trusted friend. You can create a safe space for yourself by "bookending" with a trusted friend or loved one. Call him or her to say, "I'm going to be working on some personal writing that will take me into some dark places for the next twenty minutes, so I'm going to call you to check in when I'm finished." Doing that will help you return fully to the present at the end of your writing session. You may feel safest in a place where there are other people around, a coffeehouse or a booth in a restaurant. If so, do your writing there.

Now turn your mind to remembering. Look into the eyes of the child you were and see if you can remember how you were feeling when that photo was taken. What happened that day? What were the smells in the room or the space around you? What do you remember hearing? What were you feeling? Were you sad? Angry? Worried? Hopeful? Afraid?

Take as much time as you need to think about this time in your life. When you feel ready, get out your notebook and pen and begin to write your story with your dominant hand, knowing the arm and fingers doing the writing grew from the child who was abused. Please do all this writing in longhand, not with a computer. The story you will tell will be both a memory of the past and a marker of where you are now.

The story I'd like you to begin writing should describe exactly what you remember today of:

1. Any and all physical, emotional, and sexual abuse you experienced
2. Any related memories you might have

I'd also like you to describe:

3. How the abuse affected you, which may include low self-esteem, addictions, relationships, and self-sabotaging behavior

HOW TO BEGIN

Start by labeling a page in your notebook "Physical Abuse," and write about that, if it applies to you. When you're finished, write down the details of emotional abuse and sexual abuse under new headings. In each category, try to remember the facts of the abuse. Search your memory, go back in time in your mind, and remember the who, where, when, and what.

- Who abused you?
- When did this abuse event happen?
- Where did this abuse event happen?
- What happened during this abuse event?

If you need a structure for remembering, try moving chronologically and writing about events in the order they happened. The important thing is to capture the memories as they come. You may write down an event and suddenly remember another event that happened before it. You may want to add a detail you just remembered. That's fine. You can reorder your writing. You can edit a little bit and improve the detail and the structure. Don't aim to sound like a professional memoirist. Instead, focus on remembering events as truthfully as you can and writing them down as completely as you can. Don't rush. Deliberately slowing yourself down will give your mind the opportunity to remember the past with clarity.

Many of my clients have shut down their feelings to a great extent and don't encounter much, if any, emotion as they put their stories on paper. But if you begin to feel your stress system activating—heart pounding, stomach clenching, anxiety—while you're writing, stop. Return your attention to what you're experiencing in the room right now. Breathe deeply and turn your head slowly, noticing what's on the walls. Touch your fingers together and notice their smoothness, and the temperature of your hands. If you want to stop writing for the day, stop. If you feel calmer, pick up your pen once again.

I know this may be difficult, but you can do it. "When I started to write my story, I often felt as though someone was choking me," remembered Terry, the legal secretary who was physically and sexually abused. "I couldn't wear turtlenecks, and I had horrible TMJ. Those were tangible realities of what it was like at the beginning. I was afraid, and I didn't know why. It's hard to realize that this is your *story* and it's not physically happening to you right now. Every instinct in me wanted to block it out.

"But I knew if I didn't look at my past, I wouldn't have a full and rich life. So I made myself keep going. Writing my story was a huge first step."

Take that step yourself. Write the facts without minimizing anything, and without making excuses for the abuser. Do your best to write about exactly what happened without inserting too much judgment of the past events. Our goal here is "just the facts." Just document what happened.

Instead of writing "She just slapped me once," write "She slapped me." Instead of saying, "He didn't fuck me or anything, just fondled me a couple of times," stick with, "He fondled me." Don't judge or analyze what happened. Stick with the facts.

You may be used to telling your story with commentary and qualifiers such as "It was no big deal" or "I'm sure he didn't mean it" or "It wasn't that bad." But don't use those words here. Be as straightforward as you can. Your job is to be true to your child. What really happened to that small, innocent person in the photo?

Carry the story into the present if you need to. You may have been sexually abused as a child and, in the years since, faced ongoing emotional and verbal abuse from the same person. Those experiences count as events of abuse too.

This will be a work in progress. You're going to add notes and scribble in the margins and then write another draft and start all over again as memories come to you. That's exactly the way it goes.

LOOKING AT THE EFFECTS

After you document the facts of your abuse, record the effects this abuse had on you then and how it has affected your personal, emotional, and work life in the years since—all the way up to the present. You may not want to look at your life through this lens and see what's been warped or distorted by the trauma's aftereffects. But no matter what reservations you have, keep writing.

If you're confused about where to begin, start by listing the facts of your life today:

- What is your relationship status? Are you married, divorced, single? What have your relationships with other people been like?

- Where do you live? Where do your abuser(s) live? How often have you moved?
- What kind of job do you have? Have you always had this job? What kind of career and education path have you had? Do you overwork or work too little?

And so on. You may not know everything about what happened to you or even what goes on behind your back today. The timeline in your mind may be fuzzy or have big gaps. That's okay. Write what you *do* remember, and what you know today. You'll be opening the door for the insights, understanding, and memories that will come as we continue this work.

IT MAY TAKE TIME TO FEEL

In my therapy groups, I ask people to bring their stories with them to every session and read them aloud every time someone new comes for the first time. The newcomer listens to them all before reading his or her own story by way of introduction. The experience of abuse is isolating. It's the terrible family secret, and often it's the abused child's secret shame. So it's liberating, as well as tragic and infuriating, to begin to see how that secret is shared by so many other people.

It's often difficult, especially at first, to feel the full emotional impact of your story—most people learn to live with the facts of their abuse by speeding past the pain in one way or another. Bill, the accountant who was the son of teenage addicts, did it by literally racing through his story any time he told it. He's a gentle and sweet man, but there was a disconnect between what had happened to him and the way he described it. His story, which he could tell in two minutes flat, was like a lecture in a psychology class—intense and detailed. And he was reporting and talking so fast he didn't have time to take a breath and have a feeling. He kept himself running through life so he wouldn't get bogged down in the pain.

But something opened in him as he listened to other people describe what had happened to them as children. We may be numb to our own pain, but it's difficult for any of us to hear about a child being neglected, beaten, raped, or ridiculed without a visceral feeling of injury and outrage.

Imagine you are sitting in one of my group sessions sitting in our circle, listening with us to the following stories. They may have details that resemble something that happened to you. Read with an open heart and compassion for what happened to the children whose lives are being described. If you find that doing so stirs up emotions that feel overpowering to you, please stop, and seek the support of a group or therapist who will help you address those feelings in a safe way.

Your story is powerful. The details that have brought you so much pain, despair, and confusion are a map to your healing. Take courage from the following stories, and write.

ROSE'S STORY

Rose, a buttoned-up Latina with sad brown eyes, came to me after she had an intense reaction to a first date. "I'm in a twelve-step program, Overeaters Anonymous, and I became abstinent and lost my weight," she told me. "I had been overweight for a long time, and part of being thin was to start dating. I felt very uncomfortable with the idea, but I went out with a guy, and a strange thing happened. I became practically catatonic. I did not eat or speak or say anything practically the whole time. I didn't eat for a few days after—which was so strange for me, because I use food to feel better."

The man didn't do anything alarming, she said. She explained, "I just felt unsafe. I also felt this attraction to be around him, even though I felt unsafe. It was like there was a magnet. I started feeling like I was in love with him. It was so bizarre." Rose's sponsor thought the reaction might have something to do with abuse in her past—which Rose had shared with her in step work—and gave her my number.

When I asked Rose to write her story, she told her sponsor how nervous she was about taking on the assignment, and bookended her writing sessions by calling before and after to check in. The sponsor suggested Rose go to a safe place to write, around other people, so she took herself to a Starbucks each time she worked on her story, and stayed until she had finished each section.

This is the completed story Rose brought me:

SEXUAL ABUSE

I was approximately 4 years old when I was sexually abused by a man named M. at my family's apartment. For some reason I ended up alone in the bedroom with this man. I vaguely remember him putting me on the bed and removing my panties. My next memory is when I was approximately 5-6 years old. I remember going to visit my Aunt Mara, who lived in a house nearby. I was in the backyard playing with my sister and cousins when I went into the guest room attached to the garage, where a family friend lived. I vaguely remember going into the room and M. touched me inappropriately. I don't remember the specifics.

When I was approximately 7 years old, we moved to a house in the suburbs. My cousin Richard came to live with us after he arrived from Puerto Rico. My sisters and I used to play kissing games with him. I am not sure how the kissing escalated to sexual fondling. He used to put his hands in my panties and penetrate my vagina with his fingers. I vaguely remember these things and am not sure how often the sexual molestation took place. I really cannot remember the frequency. Other memories I have of inappropriate behavior with relatives: One night when my Aunt Mara was living with us, I rubbed my body on top of her. On another occasion I was playing with my Uncle Eddie and I ended up on top of him and he rubbed himself on me when we were alone in the guest room near the garage.

PHYSICAL ABUSE

I witnessed years and years of physical abuse toward my mother and sisters. My earliest memory I have is my dad pulling a .357 magnum revolver on my mom's head and him threatening her that he was going to kill her. My father would beat my mother, siblings and me. I was my dad's favorite, so I would only get hit once or twice while my sisters would get hit three to four times more than I did. There were times we had black and blue bruises on our arms and legs. My father was careful not to hit us where other people could see. I used to get beat for many reasons or no reason at all. I would get hit for not praying or not washing dishes. I used to get hit for having a messy room. My dad used to hit me more when he was drunk.

Other types of physical abuse were unusual punishments such as kneeling on uncooked beans for hours until the beans left marks on my knees. I also have a memory of my Aunt Sophia taking care of my sisters and me. She punished me by pouring salt on my sister Maria's back and had me lick it off. I also remember my mom slapping me across the face because I wanted to go play with the neighbor's son. She said no and I insisted and she ended up slapping me like if I was a prostitute or going to do something sexual with the boy.

My father used to beat me with his leather belt with a metal belt buckle, cable wire, broom or anything he could get his hands on. I also watched him several times when he would pull a knife on my sister Maria. There were times he would pull Maria's hair and drag her all over the concrete patio until she bled. My dad once cut Maria's hair right before picture day. He chopped her hair off and forced her to take the school picture with her hair uneven. I used to get hit if men asked me to dance at a family party, if the food was not served timely on the table, making too much noise, not getting my dad's slippers, not cleaning the house, not cooking and so on . . .

EMOTIONAL ABUSE

I was a victim of verbal abuse and my mother and sisters too. My father would call me a *"puta"* [whore] all the time. He told me I was good for nothing and that one day I would grow up to clean toilets like my mother. He would call me *"pendeja, estupida, gorda, pedazos de mierda"* [a coward, stupid, fat, piece of shit] *Hija de puta*—whore's daughter. When my dad would come home from work we had to be silent and not speak. If we made any noise we would get yelled at or beat. In many ways I felt like I constantly had to walk on eggshells in fear of my dad's reaction. I experienced the emotional abuse until age 25 when I finally moved out of my parents' house for good.

MEMORIES

Some of my memories have come to me in my dreams. I also did timeline therapy and hypnosis. After that therapy, I realized that my dreams were actually real events that happened to me. I have unconsciously blocked most memories of my childhood and upbringing. I remember vague details of my childhood. It seems that every attempt I make to remember my childhood only seems to remember the bad and uncomfortable events. The little I do remember is also vague in details.

EFFECTS

The effects on my life have been many which include anxiety, intimacy and sexual issues in relation to men and self-worth. I was an insecure child and have continued through adulthood being insecure. I rarely expressed how I felt and repressed my feelings by overeating and workaholism. I did not learn to take care of myself and set healthy boundaries with people. I have been promiscuous and dissociate during sexual relations. I battle mild depression and low self-worth.

HOW DOES ROSE'S STORY MAKE YOU FEEL?

As you read Rose's story, what emotions does it bring up in you? If you've had an experience like Rose's, or that of another person whose story you read, the feeling of your experience will well up in you as you see similar details. Not the feeling of "Oh, that poor person," but the fear, the confusion that you lived with when you faced your own abuse.

What, in particular, did you relate to in Rose's story? In my therapy groups, after we listen to a person's story, we go around the room, with each member saying what felt familiar to him or her. I'd like you to go through Rose's story and imagine Rose is sitting in the room with you. Tell her out loud what parts of her story you related to. The panic, the terror, the sense of anger and powerlessness that come up when children are abused are familiar to everyone who has been through it.

For instance, Rose said her cousin moved into her family home when she was just seven years old, and "My sisters and I used to play kissing games with him. I am not sure how the kissing escalated to sexual fondling." You might tell Rose: "I felt confused too when I thought I was playing a game and all of a sudden it became sexual. I didn't know what was happening."

You may relate to the feeling of helplessness that comes with watching a family member being harmed when Rose talks about watching her sister being beaten and dragged. You might tell her, "I felt angry and afraid too." You may feel guilt at being the "chosen one" who was "only" beaten one time while others were beaten more. And you may feel sad or angry for Rose. It's fine to say, "I'm sorry you were hurt like that" or "I'd love to go hit your father right now."

EVERY KIND OF ABUSE IS SIGNIFICANT

One reason I catalog the types of abuse and ask people to write about each one is to keep you from discounting something that happened to you because you've been told, overtly or tacitly, that it's "not important."

"I was abused by many people," Rose told me early on. "Other therapists focused on the beatings and the drinking, my being around my dad, who was an alcoholic. But I had a family friend and an uncle who sexually abused me too, and it still boggles me that we didn't talk about it. I even went to family therapy with my sister, mom, and brother, and the sexual stuff was a taboo—we never said anything about it. I remember disclosing it, but I never thought it was a big deal, that it didn't affect me the way the beating and the verbal abuse did."

As you work on your story, write down whatever you remember.

Don't skip over anything because someone gave you the idea it "doesn't count." Every bit of abuse is a very big deal.

A SECOND EXAMPLE: ED'S STORY

Ed was struggling with alcohol and drug addiction when he came to see me. He sought me out after a time in his life when, as he put it, "I lost my sobriety, went to rehab, lost my relationship, my home, my whole life." He, like Rose and so many of my other clients, had focused on treating his addictions, but peace eluded him until he began looking at the abuse he had faced as a child. This is the story he brought in:

SEXUAL ABUSE

I was molested by my half-brother Don and older nephew Freddie starting as early as 6 years old. I was coerced into giving them oral sex, and they promised that in return they would give it to me. I don't think they ever did.

My brother Don didn't live with us but came to visit every holiday and summer. I remember being scared and excited for him to come. I convinced myself I was in love with him and wanted to be a girl so I could marry him. He was mean and hateful toward me and 7 years older. His penis was huge, and he made me feel small and unworthy of sexual attention. I was only 6. This fantasy relationship lasted until my brother refused to have sex with me, calling me a faggot and repelling in disgust. I was 10 years old.

At that point, Freddie took over. He would make me suck his penis while his younger brother watched. This happened from age 10 to 14. He again had a large penis and made me feel inferior and unworthy of sexual reciprocation.

During high school, I had sex with girls to prove I was not gay. I was terrified I had AIDS from my childhood abuse. In college, I began to drink and go to gay bars. I was very promiscuous and almost always dated older, more powerful men. I would make them perform and do for me, but I was disgusted to reciprocate, until I found drugs. Drugs made me feel sexually free and powerful. I felt attractive and in control.

At age 29, I was raped in my home and contracted HIV. For days, I used to dissociate and disappear, waking up in violent and horrible sexual scenarios I couldn't get out of.

PHYSICAL ABUSE

My mother yelled a lot, screamed at the top of her lungs, so loud my ears would ring. My father didn't hit me a lot, but when he did, he was usually drunk and would make me pull my pants down and make me count the beatings. He would tell me it hurt him more than it hurt me. My mom would threaten and dig her nails into me until she broke skin. My parents fought over whether I should go to the doctor when I was sick. I was sick a lot and almost died of pneumonia because they refused to take me to the doctor. I spent weeks in the hospital recovering at the age of 4.

EMOTIONAL ABUSE

Constant fighting and name-calling: "bitch, bastard, son of a bitch, faggot, homo, pansy." My mother was a seething monster who shared her most disturbing sexual personal details with me my whole life. My sister left home when I was 5, leaving me with my mother and father. I'd pray every night to die in my sleep, because I didn't know why they had me.

My parents separated when I was 7, because my father's sister and [her] husband had molested my brother Don. My mother confronted him and them, and my brother was called a liar and a troublemaker. He was being molested while he was molesting me in our own house.

My whole life, I was treated like property by my family and felt I had no rights. I had learning disabilities, and my mother moved with me to Los Angeles when I was 14 because they had better programs for me. My parents divorced. My mother blamed me for the loss of her career and marriage. She abused me emotionally by making me her husband and best friend. She told me my sister and father had an "affair" behind her back. She was paranoid and depressed. I paid the bills and took on all the adult responsibilities. My father let me live with her to shut her up. He took all the money and the houses and left her with nothing but me. She hated it. She would say I was all she had and tell me she couldn't live without me. Then she would get a boyfriend, and I would become invisible.

MEMORIES

I can't remember any more specifics about my childhood.

WHAT DO YOU RELATE TO IN ED'S STORY?

You may not have faced the same kinds of abuse Ed did, but I'm certain that elements of it will ring true to you. What did you see and hear in his story that brings up the feelings of your own experience? Perhaps you felt the same confused hope he did when he said, "I convinced myself I was in love with [my abuser]." Maybe your abuser told you, "This hurts me more than it hurts you," or you know the feeling of being "treated like property" or having to take on "all the adult responsibilities."

If Ed were sitting next to you now, what would you tell him? You might begin by saying: "I felt burdened/overwhelmed/insignificant/ angry too." Speak your answers to Ed aloud. Tell him what you relate to in his story.

Steven found the process of hearing and responding to other people's stories to be especially effective. "So often you hear, 'Get over it, move on,' when you say you had a tough childhood. But sharing our stories gives us an opportunity to mourn what has occurred, which is so tragic for so many," he said. "You wonder, 'How could that have occurred? What kind of monster could do that to a kid?' It's a chance to process something you couldn't possibly have understood at the age when it occurred. You can let down your defenses and mourn the loss of your child. And in doing that, you can *really* move on and not be tied to that past."

YOU ARE PART OF A COMMUNITY OF SURVIVORS

Everyone whose stories you see in these pages did the same work you are doing to leave behind the effects of abuse. You are part of their community, and they've offered the details of their lives and the work they did as a way of reaching out to you. Please honor them by putting the same honesty and commitment you've seen in their stories into the one you are writing. I know how difficult it is. And I want you to do it anyway.

Remember there's no comparison or competition. Mike, a forty-year-old graphic artist, remembered: "I went into the group as a newcomer and listened to everyone else's stories before I read mine. Their stories sounded so clear and concise and relatable, and I felt so inadequate. I judged myself and felt like I'd done my story wrong. But everyone would go around and tell you what they related to. You feel safe and okay when you know what we all have in common." Trust that you are writing the best version of the story you can at this moment.

Now go back to your story and your photo of the child you were. Category by category, think about what happened to that child.

You might know well the facts of your story. However, what you may not know is how your story has affected you. You might find it easy to say, "I have low self-esteem" or "I sabotage myself," but to truly examine the effects, you need to document the causes. To understand your reality today, you need to see the truth of your past, which has deeply affected your soul, the child within you.

As you go, pay attention to what the child inside you is experiencing now. If he or she is afraid, let the healthy adult part of yourself step in to offer comfort. You are safe, and the child is in the care of a good, loving parent.

The work we will do will help you examine the continued lies you may believe, even though you know the actuality of your story. You can "know" you were "raped by your father" and you can "know" you were "beaten by your mother," but you may still believe the lies: "I'm no good. I'm the bad person, and something's wrong with me. This would not have happened if only I had not provoked my abuser." Remembering the facts is a first step toward uncovering the beliefs that are still harming you. Try to keep this in mind as you write.

YOU CAN FIND THE TRUTH IN WHAT YOU HAVE NOT YET SPOKEN

A woman in my group was recovering from childhood abuse and trauma, and wanted to go home for Christmas. Her family was highly respected in her town and often honored by their church. Everyone would often speak of how wonderful this large family was, with its amazing, thriving kids, who all lived at home until they were married. My client, a recovering alcoholic, always "knew" her true story, yet she clung to the shiny, happy version, believing it would make her feel better. She had been fighting sadness for a long time and told me her grief came out when she went home for the holidays, when the "shit hit the fan" again, as it always did. Some kind of verbal abuse or emotional abuse always took place, and her brother threatened her.

So I asked her to write the facts about what happened in her life and tell the truth about how she had been treated. The truth is: Her father would grab her by the hair and beat her head against the wall. The truth is: Once her brother knocked her down the stairs, and nobody cared. The truth is: One brother fucked her, and she told her mother—and her mother turned her back. The truth is: When she told her father about the rape later in life, he said, "Lay it at the feet of Jesus."

Write your truths as honestly as this woman wrote hers.

KNOW YOUR STORY WILL CHANGE

The little person inside you is weighed down with so much darkness, he or she may not yet know how to reach out of it. If you feel something has happened to you, and you're not quite sure yet what it was, write that down too: "I don't have a clear memory, but I feel that there was some kind of sexual [or other] abuse." You're opening a door to memory, and to the clarity that will come in time.

ASSIGNMENT 1: Finish Your Writing

Complete a draft of your story, seeking all the support you need as you write. As you go, remind yourself of where you are at this moment: *You are safe in the present, no longer in the middle of the abuse.* This is a good time to talk to your inner child. Let him or her know everything is going to be okay.

ASSIGNMENT 2: Record Yourself Reading Your Story Aloud

When you have finished writing, please put your pen down. Walk away. Take as much time as you need. I understand fully how difficult this task has been. But you did it, and you're doing it. You are honoring the commitment letter that you wrote to your child in the last chapter. Keep your child close as you work to heal him or her. You are together, and the truth will set you both free. When you are ready, please record yourself reading your story aloud. It will be valuable to listen to it later in this process.

5

WHAT TO DO WITH THE FEELINGS

For many people, writing their story for the first time and hearing themselves speak it aloud cracks open the door to the hidden past. When you listen to yourself reading it, you may notice that your telling seems almost clinical, without a lot of feeling. It may be a jumble of details that doesn't quite cohere. The pain that's so apparent when you read other people's stories may not be apparent to you the first time you write down your own. It's normal for that to happen when the emotions of abuse are still stored separately from the facts inside you.

But you may also be hit with the gut-punch realization that the small child in the picture, the child who was you, was hurt in ways you hadn't allowed yourself to admit. That's normal too. The reality seeps in, in different ways for everyone.

"At first, I thought my story wasn't so bad," said Steven. "But when I sat with the picture of my kid and wrote it out, it was hard not to hear or see how horrific it was. Listening to someone else talk about what happened to them, I've thought, 'My God. How terrible. You poor kid.' Sometimes I want to just get up and go punch someone's mother in the face for doing that to her own son. It didn't take long for me to realize things were that bad for me too. It's easier to think it's normal until someone points out that what happened isn't what most kids go through.

"Soon you see that it's not normal for a mother to wash your mouth out with soap. It's not normal to be left with an uncle who has sex with you. You know that automatically when you hear someone else's story. And then you begin to know it about yours."

These are big, painful connections to make. Rose, whose story you saw in the last chapter, was unemotional when she first talked about the terror of being in her house when she was growing up.

She said, "At nine o'clock, that's when my hell started. My dad would beat us, and we'd have to run for our lives and go to a gas station so Dad wouldn't find us. And then I'd go to school the next morning. I'd have to show up and do well when I was up till two, three, four a.m. being hit. My body was black-and-blue, and I would wear long-sleeve shirts so teachers wouldn't notice I was being beat. I was scared shitless. I couldn't sleep."

But when she read her story to her therapy group, other people's eyes welled up with sadness—and hers did too. The whole, healthy adult part of her imagined the child's experience and began to connect with the emotions underlying the words that had described the events. Her child's pain stayed at the front of her mind. "Now I see my friends with their children, and notice how loving and caring they are," she told me sadly. "They help their kids put on their jammies and brush their teeth and have their milk and cookies, read them a story. I didn't have that."

As you begin to take in what happened in your past, every kind of emotion can arise: longing for the love and care you did not have. Anger at the people who inflicted pain instead of offering love and comfort. Layers of sadness for the child who deserved tenderness, support, and affirmation and faced hell instead.

Though you may have spent years trying to numb these emotions and push them away when they flared into your awareness, I want you to treat them differently this time. I'll show you how to deal with the feelings that have always felt too hot to touch, and to do it in a way that will let you protect yourself without walling off the emotional truths that will allow you to heal. Your feelings will guide you, transform you, and lead you to recovery if you keep working with them rather than running from them again.

That's why it's important to me that you have the resources that will allow you to do that. For the long haul, throughout the process, use the basic tool kit in this chapter to stay safe, soothed, and present as you begin to open yourself to the feelings of the child inside.

A TECHNIQUE FOR COMING INTO THE PRESENT

Looking at the stories of your abuse may confuse and panic the child inside you, who has never believed the abuse is over. Now, the details laid out clearly as never before, you may feel overpowered, as though the danger the child faced in the past is right here.

Anytime this happens, put any work you're doing with this book aside and breathe slowly and deeply, emphasizing a long exhale. Breathe the air of freedom from your past. You are no longer in danger. You are no longer the helpless child who must rely on adults to provide your most basic needs. You are in charge. You are safe. And you can keep yourself and your child safe.

You are the adult now.

Repeat this practice, which I hope will become a habit: Put your feet on the ground and feel yourself right here. Notice what the air smells like. Run your fingers over a nearby surface and experience the texture of your desk or couch or the inside of your arm. Notice the details of the room around you, the colors and sounds. If you have a cup of coffee beside you, pick it up and feel the surface and temperature of the cup. Take in the aroma of the coffee. You are here. You are safe. Breathe. You are safe. Pay attention to the way your breath causes your chest to rise and fall. Feel your feet on the floor and the way the earth supports you.

If you have a warm-blooded pet—a dog or cat or fuzzy hamster—it can be extremely calming and grounding to stroke and play with this companion, feeling its bond with you, and its presence.

REMEMBER: SEEK SUPPORT IF YOU FEEL OVERWHELMED

It's your job to take the best care you can of the child inside you. If you sense yourself becoming overwhelmed, please seek the help of a therapist, therapy group, or other support group. The people whose stories you read in this book drew tremendous comfort and courage from being in a group setting, where they could share their experiences in a safe environment. Create a list of people you can call if you need to—your therapist, your twelve-step sponsor, your partner, a caring friend who believes you. Turn to them for support when you need it. You don't have to do this alone.

A POWERFUL BREATHING EXERCISE TO GROUND AND COMFORT YOU ANY TIME YOU NEED IT

I learned this simple exercise from Dr. Andrew Weil, who recommends doing it any time you're upset, tense, or anxious: Breathe in through your nose to the count of four, hold your breath for a count of seven, and then breathe out to the count of eight by blowing out the air in a smooth flow. Dr. Weil keeps the count steady, and not particularly slow, and suggests doing this four-seven-eight breathing three times in a row.

Try it and see how you feel. If you want to do it again, go ahead.

My clients use it to help them fall asleep, to help interrupt racing thoughts, and to create a feeling of calm. It's always there for you, a gift you can always give yourself, and your upset child.

CREATE A SAFE SPACE FOR YOURSELF AND THE CHILD

When you were small, you didn't have a safe place to go. The home that was supposed to be your sanctuary was instead full of danger. Now you can change that. I'd like you to create a "safe place" in your home that you can think of as a space for regrouping as you do this work. It can be a room, or just part of one, where you can retreat into safety and comfort. It might just be a place on your bed that has something you like to hold—a soft blanket, a special pillow, a stuffed animal. Little children know what they're doing when they carry around toys or blankets that give them an extra sense of security. Objects like that bring us back into ourselves rather than letting us float into the anxieties of another time and place.

Any time you're in your safe place, tell yourself: "It's right now, not the past, and right now everything is fine. I am strong and healthy. In this moment I am safe. Nothing from the past can hurt me. I'm wrapped in comfort and safety. I'm wrapping my child in love."

THE PRACTICE THAT WILL FREE YOU: GO TO THE CHILD

When your body feels calmer, be sure to tend to the child. I realize your relationship with the child inside you is new and may feel tenuous or even "faked" at this point. But whether you feel close to the child or distant right now, your job is to keep looking at your photo of the child and do your best to imagine that version of yourself as if he or she were in the room with you. When you feel upset, know the child is upset. Reach out to offer comfort to the child any time you feel an outsized emotion. The child feels everything with great intensity. And it's within your power to find out exactly what is upsetting him or her, and to offer relief.

I know you are used to running for the exit doors when tough feelings come up. Many of you have self-medicated with alcohol, drugs, food, or sex. You may be like Bill, who describes himself as "an escape artist" who was always seeking a way out through one of his addictive behaviors any time his pain surfaced. Even when he was sober in his twelve-step programs, he was inclined to tunnel away from the pain.

Now, instead of checking out by turning on the TV, disappearing into the Internet, masturbating, reaching for a bag of chips, shopping, or turning to another one of your usual escape routes, I want you to reach for the child first. Stop, take a deep breath, and look for your child whenever you're hurting. *To help yourself, help your child.*

Bill learned to do this by asking himself: "If someone I truly loved were having these feelings, what would I do for them? What would I say?" Sometimes, he said, that meant "being alone when I need to be alone, or being with people, or just resting. I feel like I'm making room for what that part of me needs, instead of pretending he doesn't exist and putting my attention somewhere else. The child is shockingly honest, and I'm getting to know what he wants."

APPROACH YOUR CHILD WITH COMFORTING WORDS

If you feel a rush of anger or sadness, write to the child and tell him or her what a good parent would say on noticing a child was upset. You don't have to use these exact words, but say something like this:

Dear [little one],

I know you're feeling sad/scared/angry. I promise you I will stay with you and protect you no matter what. You're safe with me. I will not let anyone hurt you.

Do you want to talk about what you're scared/angry/worried about?

I love you very much, and I'm here to take care of you.

Love,

[your name]

Now use right hand/left hand to see if the child has anything to tell you. Use your dominant hand to ask: "How are you feeling?" "What would make you feel better?" "Is anything else bothering you?"

Use your nondominant hand to let the child answer. You may get a one- or two-word answer. That's fine. The child may simply write "Sad" or "I'm scared." Be sure to listen and then *respond*, using your dominant hand. You can say something like, "Honey, I am sorry you are sad. I'm here for you. You're here with me. I'm sad too about what happened, but I am happy we are together. I will take care of you. I love you." Sign your note "Mom" or "Dad."

If the child writes nothing, write a note reassuring him or her that it's okay, that you are listening, and that you are there.

It may take a dozen or a hundred "I love you. I am here for you" notes to demonstrate to the child that you are actually there, and that it's safe to trust that you will continue to be. Just keep showing up and writing loving words to him or her anytime your emotions feel overwhelming. Don't let the child stand suffering in front of you. Scoop that child up and wrap him or her in comforting words and actions.

And don't be surprised when the child, in telling you what will make him or her feel better, tells you exactly what you need to do.

Here's a short exchange Rose had with her little girl not long after she had written her story and began feeling anxious and overwhelmed.

Dear Little Rose,

How are you feeing today? Do you feel taken care of?

Love,
Mom

Dear Mom,

I am feeling angry. I feel like life is too much and hard. I am tired.

Love,
Little Rose

When Rose shared these notes in her group session, the other women pointed out that while she had asked her little girl for her feelings, she had not responded when Little Rose offered them. Rose was crestfallen. "I feel terrible," she said. "It will take practice for me to listen to my inner child. I think I've ignored her for so long that it's second nature to me."

Just recognizing that tendency gives you the opportunity to change, and to learn to be kind to the child. Again, that's why we call this work parenting class. You weren't taught to be a good parent—you're going to make mistakes. Rose did what you can do any time you realize you haven't fully responded to your child: She apologized and tried again.

Dear Little Rose,

I am sorry for not acknowledging your feelings. I am practicing being a better parent. I am learning. What can I do for you? How can I comfort your pain?

Love,
Mom

Dear Mom,

I have a lot of pain inside. I am tired. I want you to take care of me. Please don't ignore. Love me.

Little Rose

The child's words will open your heart, and they can guide you. Write to your child, listen to the child, and do your best to give the child what he or she requests when you know it will serve both of you. This is your fallback: Go to the child.

I know it will take time and practice to begin to do this. Remember to calm your physical body first, then talk to the child. All the tools I've collected here will help you and the child feel better.

USE STROKING AND TAPPING TO GIVE YOUR CHILD COMFORT

One of the most comforting things you can do for yourself when your emotions feel overwhelming is to hug your child, just as you longed to be hugged when you were little and felt sad or afraid. Wrap your arms around yourself, embracing the child you were. You might gently pat your shoulder or back as your arms encircle you. You can say, "Everything's all right. I'll take care of you"—or whatever words you would've wanted to hear when you were upset.

We humans naturally calm ourselves with touch. It's the first sense to develop, and it connects us both to other people and ourselves. Offering the comfort of touch to your child can be as simple as stroking your arm gently while saying, aloud or silently, "It's all right. Everything's all right now. You're safe. I'm taking care of you."

You can do this any time, in any setting, without feeling as though you're calling attention to yourself, and it's deeply soothing. A traditional Chinese treatment for sadness is to massage the arms or to run a palm over the smooth skin on the inside of the forearm using long strokes from the wrist toward the shoulder. Such stroking stimulates acupuncture points associated with grief, and while I can only tell you from personal experience that it's calming, numerous studies have shown that acupuncture and tapping acupressure points can calm the stress systems of the brain. (You can Google "Emotional Freedom Techniques"—EFT—for basic information on tapping.)

My clients find it soothing to tap the thymus, which is just below the notch separating the collarbones. You can tap that spot with a finger, or, as some suggest, pound it lightly with a fist.

Breathe deeply as you use these soothing techniques, and reassure the child that you're there to protect him or her.

GRIEF HAS TO HAVE SOMEWHERE TO GO

Some people who are taking a new look at their story think the adult thing to do is wipe their tears away and get on with life. I often hear clients say, "I don't want to wallow in my sadness. I don't want to feel sorry for myself, and I don't want any pity."

But you're not feeling sorry for *yourself* when grief rises in you in response to your memories of abuse. You're feeling sorry for the child—and your child deserves that sympathy. Your child is entitled to your sorrow and your pity, your regret for what he or she had to endure.

You have a right to cry for this child. All the grief you've tried to walk away from is still there inside you, and your tears are a way of letting your buried grief surface so you can release it. Visual reminders of your child—how small he or she actually was, how vulnerable—will help you free your feelings, and being around children who are the age you were in your photo may connect you to your memories and your tears. It's okay to cry.

Jennifer cried for months to release all the grief she'd locked up inside. "As the sadness is coming up," she told me, "a lot comes from seeing things from a different point of view. I look at my photos of little Jenny, and then I'll be with my niece, who's seven now, and go, 'Oh my God. She's just a little girl. She's so innocent.' And I think about what happened to me when I was that small. Sometimes I can't stop crying, because my little girl should have been protected. None of this was her fault. And I can see that so clearly by looking at my niece."

Rose always carries a photo of her Little Rose. "I look at her picture and I think about how if someone would've shown me a photo of a little girl like that and told me all she'd been through, it would bring me to tears. My little girl has been so brave and so alone. She is amazing. And I get that when I look at her."

Jennifer and Rose cried easily for the children inside them, but some people pride themselves on staying dry-eyed and "rational." One of my clients, Ben, a forty-five-year-old businessman, wells up when he talks about what happened to him—he lived with near-constant emotional and physical abuse as a child. But he wipes his eyes roughly with the back of his hand and pulls in the tears, shutting down his feelings as suddenly as they appear.

As a result, he's a very angry guy—and he doesn't know why he's angry. He erupts at his kids and his employees, and he's got an extremely short fuse on the road, where he's always one step away from full-on rage at other drivers. Unexpressed grief has a way of turning to a kind of generalized anger at the world that only makes you feel more isolated and alone. It's as though we need our tears to wash out the emotional wounds of the abuse, and if we don't allow them to flow, the injuries fester and become inflamed. We let off the heat with misplaced anger and rage—intense feelings that are not directed at those who hurt us but at those far from the source of our pain. And when that makes life worse, many people retreat into denial and abandon the child they were. To stay with the child, and do this work, you'll have to let yourself cry.

HEALTHFUL ANGER

Ben's kind of anger—rage that's not consciously connected to the perpetrators of the abuse, the people who deserve it—doesn't help you or the child. But anger focused on those who hurt you can be healthy and healing.

If that kind of rage hits you as you think about your story, know that it's a healthy response. You have a right to be angry about what was done to you as a child. You have a right to be intensely angry. It's human to be outraged at what happened. The important thing is to channel that anger appropriately. When someone tells me their story and says, "I'm so angry I could kill my parents," I tell them, "You're not going to kill anyone. But you can release that anger in ways that will make you feel better."

Here are some ground rules for letting the anger out:

- If you want to release the energy of your anger in a physical way, choose an outlet that will not hurt anyone. Throw rocks at a wall, or hurl potatoes that will make a dramatic splat. Beat a pillow. Wail on a punching bag.
- As you do this, aim your angry words toward your abuser or non-protector. Be specific. As you throw your rock or tennis ball or potato, say, "I'm so angry at you, Mom. How dare you hit a helpless child with a wire hanger! [name the abuse]. How dare you! This will never fucking happen again."

Using words like this does a few helpful things. It acknowledges the wrong done by the perpetrator. It directs the energy of the anger at the proper target. And it tells the child: "I'm here now. I'm a powerful adult. And the abuse will never happen again."

A WRITING ASSIGNMENT FOR ANGER AND EMPOWERMENT

As well as using your body to channel anger, you can use the written word. There's something intensely freeing and restorative about putting your rage in writing. Many, many people in my groups find great release in addressing their abusers on paper by writing:

"When you _____ [did this to me], I felt _____. How dare you [do this]."

You won't be sending this to anyone, just writing—by hand—in your notebook for yourself and your child.

One of Rose's letters looked like this:

Dad,

When you hit me it made me feel like you did not love or care for me. It made me feel like I was worthless and disposable. How dare you treat me like I did not matter.

When you shouted and called me names it made me feel small and insignificant. How dare you treat me in a disrespectful manner.

Rose

Writing in this way tells your child you are not sitting silently without responding to the abuse. You are safely and directly addressing the wrong, saying it's not okay, and letting your anger out.

Feel free to do this as often as you like.

SELF-CARE IS VITAL NOW—TAKE EXCELLENT CARE OF YOURSELF

The emotional work you're doing is extremely demanding. As your feelings rise, you need to be strong to learn these new ways of dealing with them. Be sure to put basic self-care in place for yourself and your child:

- MAKE A PLAN TO EXERCISE. Physical activity is good for your overall health, but it's especially vital for raising your levels of serotonin, the "feel-good" neurotransmitter that's responsible for a runner's high and the way your mood improves after any heart-pounding workout. Stress—and this work is stressful—depletes serotonin, and it's important to have adequate serotonin levels to give yourself the perspective you need.

- FACE ANY ISSUES WITH DEPRESSION HEAD-ON. It's normal, as noted previously, to feel sad when you do this work. Sadness is nothing to be afraid of. But if you feel nothing but sadness for weeks on end, or find you feel immobilized, hopeless, or unable to take pleasure in any part of your life, please see a psychiatrist who can prescribe medication that will help keep your serotonin levels correctly balanced and restore the emotional resources you need to do this work. It's better to inform yourself than to suffer. Keep in mind that medication isn't a Band-Aid, and it's not another path to numbness. It's a focused tool that will help you work better with your past.

Many of my clients resist seeking this kind of help and, on finally agreeing to a short course of medication, tell me they wish they had tried it sooner. It often happens that depression has been your normal for so long that you don't realize how much better you could feel.

One client recently told me, "I thought that depression was you stay home and don't shower or brush teeth. I'm the opposite—a workaholic—and I didn't realize I was a highly functional depressed person. The psychiatrist I saw told me that not only was I depressed but that I'd been that way a long time. I was only sleeping four hours a night because I had so much going on, six hours at the most. And I couldn't even recognize when I was tired. Once I got medication— an antidepressant plus sleeping pills—it recalibrated me. I'd been in fight-or-flight mode for so long. No wonder I didn't sleep.

"I wish I had listened from the beginning because it's much easier to do this work now. The medication didn't solve my problems. But it's making it a lot easier to uncover and look at the difficult stuff."

If you think you might be helped by medication for depression and money is a concern, check out the free and low-cost mental health centers in your community. Many people I've worked with have used these services with good results.

- TRY YOGA. Yoga, with its focus on breathing and attention to the sensations that arise in each pose, can help you tune in to what's going on inside you and to experience your body, from which you may feel very disconnected, a safe environment. It's being studied as a treatment for trauma that could be as effective as drugs in helping people calm stress in the body, and you can find programs and videos geared to "yoga for trauma" or "trauma-sensitive yoga." I highly recommend checking them out.
- BE SURE YOU'RE EATING AND SLEEPING PROPERLY. I often see people who are so consumed by their emotional work they forget about their physical needs. Feed your child regular meals. Go to a health food store and look for supplements that offer good support for your immune and nervous systems. Replenish yourself. Rest.

- DO SOMETHING KIND FOR YOUR CHILD. Think about what you liked to do when you were little. Maybe you liked bike riding or drawing or chasing bubbles or just wandering around in a toy store looking at the toys. Maybe you have happy memories of being outside or playing with a pet. Give your child a play break. It may sound silly, but it will raise your spirits. Don't beat yourself up if you don't have ready thoughts about what your child would enjoy; just ask the child. It's fine to simply surprise your child with a small present—a box of crayons or a walk in the park. Pleasure is healing.

You're in this for the long run, so use any and every soothing technique that works for you. Lynn, the legal secretary healing from physical and sexual abuse, put it this way: "Working with my kid and my story, I do what's in front of me. You eat the elephant a bite at a time, and don't look at the whole elephant. Looking at the elephant is like, 'Oh fuck. I'll never be able to do this.' But you do, bit by bit. It's tough, so you've got to find some kind of peace wherever you can find it. I do it all—meditation, yoga, hiking, twelve-step meetings. Anything that makes me feel like I'm part of the human race for some brief time. Acupuncture, massage. I'm down for anything that will give me some relief."

That's a healthy approach, especially the focus on connecting with the body, and I hope you'll give yourself permission to use it.

Finally, remember that sometimes falling apart is falling together. Feelings will come and come in this work, and they'll challenge you. Comfort yourself in ways that don't block the feelings. Reach for your child and soothe him or her, even as you allow the feelings to flow and change and give you new information. If you stop the feelings, you'll be stuck. Have the courage to feel. I know you can do it.

Do it for yourself. Do it for your child.

6

GETTING THE CHILD'S VIEW OF WHAT HAPPENED

It's natural to want to confine your story to the facts and "get over" the feelings that it brings up, because that's the "adult" thing to do. We cling to the idea that our story is over, that the past is the past. Now that you've got your story on paper, and have calmed any initial feelings that arose when you wrote down what happened to you, you might be inclined to simply put your memories back in the drawer. You might even consider yourself to be one of the "lucky" ones who managed to avoid anger or tears, and be telling yourself that that's proof you've done all you need to.

The rational side of you that's been managing your life would simply like to get on with things. But the child can't and won't—all the aftereffects of abuse you're experiencing are the child's way of letting you know that. It's the child's emotional reactions to the facts of your story that are running your life. So we need to make it safe for the feelings about the abuse to surface, and to integrate them by learning what the child is feeling and experiencing.

We'll do that in two ways: First, you'll go to the child and ask for his or her memories of what the abuse was like. Then I'll teach you a practice for learning to recognize when the child is reacting in the present to feelings from the past, and help you address those feelings directly, rather than letting them continue to trigger automatic responses.

ASKING FOR THE CHILD'S VERSION OF THE STORY

When Grace, a tense forty-five-year-old math teacher, came to see me, she'd been pushing away her past for a long time. Her parents had split up when she was three and she'd been left in the care of her father. He remarried the next year, and her new stepbrother, Jacob, who was ten years old, began to molest her. Grace's stepmother beat her when Grace approached her for help, and her father sided with his new family. Grace went to live with an aunt at the age of sixteen and went through therapy in her twenties. She believed she'd put the abuse behind her, but recently her life seemed to be falling apart. She wanted to find out why.

"I was able to control everything until I was in my early forties," she told me. "I was highly functional, I had a great marriage and friends, I was successful in my job. But then my husband came into a lot of money and I stopped having to work. I began premenopause, and those hormonal changes began to trigger devastating memories for me—flashbacks of what happened with my stepbrother."

During that time, Grace started drinking heavily and regularly getting high on pot. "I can't take it anymore," she told me. "I cry all the time and I'm angry and irritated with the slightest things and with everyone around me. I pulled away from my husband and stopped having sex with him. I've cut off my friends. I don't even answer the phone because I can't talk to anyone. I'm basically shutting down all my relationships because I can't deal with anyone, and I just stay in my house, feeling alone and angry."

She'd called me, she said, because, "I'm really losing it. I've started going to AA meetings, but when I come home, I just sit on my couch watching hours and hours of TV. I've got it down to one movie in particular: *The Parent Trap*, the original and the remake. I've been watching the reruns over and over and over."

Grace told me she knew exactly what had happened to her as a child. She had read enough books on abuse and talked about it enough with previous therapists that she was clear about its effects. She just wasn't clear about why her life was crumbling or what she could do about it.

When she came to my office for our first appointment, she told me the story of her abuse for the first time. She was highly analytical, saying, "I was abused by a relative at a young age, but my core trauma was not sex abuse. It was abandonment by my mother at a very young age. That started the whole chain reaction that conditioned me to feel less than, so whenever the pedophile stepped forward, I was already conditioned to accept the abuse."

That's the way her first written description came across too.

Now she looks back and says, "I was running from my story. There were variations of it, but mostly I held on to the intellectual story, disconnected from my emotions. Yeah, I was sexually abused as a kid, and it was rough, and really, isn't that all you need to know? I'd tell people that much, but once a person stopped asking, I didn't talk anymore. I'd been married twenty years and my husband didn't really know my story, my girlfriends didn't know it. No one really did.

"So when I wrote it down, I followed the instructions to the letter, but I gave the intellectual version."

In truth, that was the only version of the story that was available to her, the story as it was understood by her logical, rational left brain.

Where were the *feelings* that belonged to Grace's story? To get access to them, we needed to go to the little girl inside.

I asked Grace to invite the little girl inside her to help her tell the story again, using her nondominant hand. "Just let the little girl tell you anything she needs to, in whatever way she can. There's no format, and she may not say much. But anything she says will be important," I said.

Grace, with a great sigh and more than a little skepticism, promised she would, and at our next session she told me the process hadn't been easy. She said, "I went home, I sat there and nothing came up whatsoever. I called my AA sponsor and told her, 'This is dumb. I don't have a "little girl." I'm not getting anything.' My sponsor said, 'Just give it twenty minutes more and call me back. Maybe your girl is just pissed at you. Maybe she doesn't want to talk to you.' So I got off the phone and started talking to my little girl, and all of a sudden I got a couple of bits—it started happening."

"Where are you, little girl?" Grace wrote with her dominant hand.

The little girl replied: "I'm hiding from you because you don't like me. You think I'm ugly and stupid and you never like anything I say or want. You don't want me around. You are mean, and I don't think you care about me. Nobody does. Nobody loves me."

Startled and stricken with guilt, Grace apologized to the little girl and reassured her that she loved her and was learning to care for her. "I know I wasn't there in the past, but I'm here now, and I'm not going anywhere," she wrote. "When I look at you, I can see that you're beautiful, and I know you're so smart." Then she asked the little girl what was going on in the house where she lived.

The child wrote, "Daddy makes me cry. Why does he always leave me? Where is Mommy? She's gone too. I feel so scared, nobody wants me. Ethan hurts me. You push me away."

"I had heard about the inner child," Grace told me after she read the child's story to me, "but I didn't believe in it and I didn't want to. I didn't believe it could work. I thought it was just something someone had made up. But I didn't make this up. It's real.

"I grew up in an environment with so many lies, where I was told to lie and threatened if I didn't. I'm really good at hiding on a deep, subconscious level," she said. "But something about this writing broke through."

If you keep writing, keep listening, the child *will* come out of hiding. Be aware that what your child feels, remembers, and notices will crack the shell that's walled off the feelings of the past. The child's words will give you access to what it felt like to endure what you had to endure, and bring you into contact with the pain your child is still experiencing. If you aren't ready to go there alone, do what Grace did and contact a therapist to work with you through this vital part. Do whatever you need to, to make yourself feel safe. Safety and love are what the child has always lacked, and as it feels them, the child can come to you.

ASSIGNMENT 1: Ask the Child to Talk About What Happened

Invite the child to share his or her memories of the abuse. Use your dominant hand to ask: "Can you tell me your story about growing up in your house? What happened to you when you were little?"

Then pick up your pen with your nondominant hand and let the child answer. Your little boy or girl will tell you the story in his or her own simple, direct language. There's no format for this evolving story, and it may come in tiny pieces. Your child may write things much like what Grace's child did: "Daddy hurt me. I love my Daddy . . . Mommy didn't help me . . . You weren't there . . . I'm mad at you." Sometimes you'll only get a word or two. However, each one will help you connect with the feelings you experienced and give you clarity about exactly what happened.

Don't try to impose a format. Just thank the child for any words he or she offers.

The child's reality may not be easy to look at, but remind yourself that you can remember this history without reexperiencing the abuse. You are in the present, safe now. The feelings and sensations in your body are changing, moment by moment. Take a second now to close your eyes and breathe. What's happening in your arms and legs? Are they heavy or light? Shake your hands. How does that feel? Feel the air coming in and out of your nose. Track the motion of your body. Every moment is different. That's the physical experience of the present.

The fear is that when difficult feelings arise, they'll last forever. But here in the present, they change, just as the sensations in your body do. If the child inside you is frightened, keep using the soothing techniques I've taught you. Today, as never before, you can comfort the child, and reassure your adult self too, that you're finally safe.

Grace got a great deal of relief when I suggested that she do the "When you did _____ to me I felt _____. How dare you do this to me?" exercise I showed you on page 96. It feels good to write it out, then read it aloud. The child longs for someone to talk back to the abuser, to say, "This hurt. It was wrong." Those words have been a long time coming, and they'll feel empowering to both you and the child.

FOLLOW THE EMOTIONS OF THE PAST THAT ECHO INTO THE PRESENT

The child is always communicating with you, and when you know what to look for, you can use the signals coming from the child to add details to your map of the past. Many times, we're triggered by something people say, or we have strong reactions to places or events—or even to the way someone looks at us. Suddenly we're enraged, or thrown into sadness or fear, and we know there's more to our response than our feelings about the actual circumstances. I'm talking about things like the fight a wife picks with her husband when he raises his eyebrows at something she says, or the way a tough guy suddenly cringes when his boss raises his voice in a conversation across the room.

We act and react as though our irrationally overblown responses are logical, simple cause and effect: "Of course I'm mad. You're making fun of me with that look." But it's impossible to deal with triggering events on a logical level because, as we've seen, they're not coming from the reasoning side of the brain. Instead, we're reading something into the situation based on the experiences of the past—and the child can point us to the deeper cause, which often goes straight to the abuse.

Many people who come to me from talk therapy say, "Of course that's what's going on. It's my past. I'm sensitive because of the abuse. We all know that. So what else is new?" They've made the connection in their minds, and it hasn't changed anything. *But they haven't ever talked to the kid.*

What I'd like you to do is to make a habit of asking for your child's input any time a situation triggers you to make a big issue of something inconsequential, or to react in a way that just doesn't fit.

The simple technique goes like this: Pay attention to what pushes your emotional buttons and gets a reaction from you that's bigger than the situation that prompted it. Make an actual note of the trigger: "the eyebrows thing" or "Sam's yelling." If you have a moment right away, stop and write to your child, asking, "When was the first time you can remember feeling this way?"

Use your nondominant hand to answer. It might be something

like: "I remember when Mommy looked at me and then hit me."

Then ask: "When was another time?" and again let the child answer with your nondominant hand.

With every answer, you'll be making links from the present to the past, and the child will help you remember more. What's important is not finding the very first time you experienced the feeling that's triggering big reactions in your life now—there's nothing particularly magical about the first time you felt a particular fear or anxiety. Change comes from beginning to connect a whole *series* of incidents to the way you react now. Taking time to notice that you're reacting, and to let the healthy adult part of you ask why by directing you to the child, builds the habit of reflection into your life. When you feel your stomach lurch when someone raises her voice near you, or your temper explodes when someone changes lanes in front of you without signaling, pay attention. As soon as you notice, get in the habit of saying, "Whoa. What just happened?" and, as quickly as you can, ask what the child remembers.

Our days aren't always constructed in a way that lets us stop to write, so if you need to, you can do your detective work after the fact, perhaps at the end of the day, when you are already checking in with your child. I might write, "Little Arlene, you had a strong reaction when that person in the elevator made a joke about our shoes. When do you remember feeling this way before?" and let the child take it from there.

WHO'S REACTING? THE CHILD OR THE ADULT?

At first, Steven was wary of stopping to check in with the child (I believe his exact words were, "Oh, give me a break."). But as he did, he began to see the child at work in his daily life. "I started to realize that, oh, that response to my boss was not an adult response. He just asked a question, he didn't attack me. You see that and you

go, 'Wait, if that's a kid who just spoke up, what would an adult do?'
That's when I got fascinated by this process."

Bill, the accountant, had a similar response: "I started out by
making little notes to myself when something came up during the
day, and I started to see that I was having these feelings that were
disproportionate to what was happening. Like that person I was
having sex with, who I didn't really know that well, decided to
end the relationship—and that would devastate me. It didn't make
sense. So in a nice, parent-y way, I would ask the kid, 'What the
heck is that about? When did you first feel like that?' The feelings
of fear or shame would be so intense, and it felt so unrelated to the
now. Like such old feelings. And the kid kept pointing to my mom.

"My kid is helping me see that it's normal for me to have people
in my life who say they're available, but they're not. My mom did
that all the time. I guess that's my kind of warped blueprint for what
love looks like."

The similarities between present and past, between new relationships and the one with his mother, became much clearer to Bill
as he tracked his big feelings of disappointment and disconnected-
ness with other people to the way he felt as a child, in a home where
his mom was physically close but emotionally far away.

Think of yourself as a person who's collecting clues that, taken
together, will reveal the shape and feeling of situations that aren't
clearly visible yet. Every time you make the connection—"Oh,
something's going on inside me, and it feels old and familiar, like
something from my past"—you and your child begin to untangle
the present from your history and integrate the understanding that
everything's okay now. You don't have to fight or run or be blindly
pulled toward people and situations that aren't good for you. You
have other choices.

The more you take care of the child, and let him or her know he
or she is safe in the present, the more you can pause, reflect, and do

interventions, such as replaying someone's comments in your mind and hearing that they're not attacks before you respond. That's not going to happen with one "aha" experience. You have to keep going back and back to the child, collecting the child's memories, becoming familiar with his or her specific experiences, providing reassurance.

Rose got her first true sense of the child's intense feelings when she was house-sitting for a friend. "I was alone in her house, and all of a sudden I wake up at night and I'm like in terror," she told me. "I did not understand what was going on. I was freaking out, I was so scared. Then I remembered how you said my little girl was going to communicate in the dark, where so many bad things happened. I hugged myself to give her a hug, and I said, 'It's okay, baby, you're safe. You're okay.' It was a miracle I could go back to bed, because it was like I'd seen a horror movie.

"This was the first time I truly believed in my little girl, even though she'd been writing to me. That fear was out of the blue, but I talked to her and calmed her down, and it worked. I get it now that any time I feel fear or anxiety or want to overeat, it's my little girl not feeling safe. It's *her*. So I've been listening to her. If I feel her getting upset, I do right hand/left hand with her. I hug her and tell her, 'Baby, I'm right here. It's okay. You'll be forever safe.' And it works."

When you can *observe* the child expressing those old feelings—fears, angers, and anxieties that don't seem to belong to the moment you're in—you can begin to connect them with what happened in the past, and disconnect them from the events of the present.

COMMIT TO PURSUING YOUR FEELINGS TO THEIR SOURCE

This is important, so let's recap:

From now on, any time you experience a strong reaction to something in your daily life, take time to calm your body. Use the self-soothing techniques that work best for you and let your heart and breathing slow down. Reassure the child that he or she is safe. Then ask:

- When did you first feel this way?
- Can you think of another time when you had this feeling?
- Where were you?
- How old were you?

Respond by writing with your nondominant hand. It is important to keep asking any questions that come up if you feel a conversation beginning. You may want to clarify something or look for more details about a memory that's beginning to surface.

Writing these questions and answers is a simple action, but I guarantee you will find these dialogues to be healing. Every day, they will change your life. You will become less reactive to the ancient feelings your child experienced during the years of abuse. You will be able to separate those emotions from the way the safe, healthy adult part of you feels in the moment. And as you practice writing about and questioning your emotions as they arise, you'll feel more congruent and find that your feelings are better matched to the situations you face. The "When did you first feel like this?" dialogue is a beautiful way to work toward self-containment: containing your child within while putting your healthy adult self in charge of the person you are today.

You don't need to turn this into a rote exercise and use the same questions the same way every day. In fact, the more you do this exercise, the more you will think of your own questions. I encourage you to ask your child whatever question you feel fits.

Please take the time to start using this technique right now, and use it whenever the need strikes. Then keep going. Make connections. Get to know what's really going on inside you.

YOU *WILL* REPARENT YOUR CHILD

Your job is to be the good parent, and you must show up so you can love, nurture, protect, and care for your child. You'll need to set strong boundaries for the child and give him or her the tools to go out into the world to become a centered, happy adult.

If your child is scared, wants to act out, or gets angry, those feelings will affect your current relationships, both personal and professional. You can make lasting changes in your life if, at those moments of disproportionate fear and anger, you pause to do some right-hand/left-hand writing.

Change comes from getting to the core of your feelings. I know that's hard, but it's essential to keep excavating those early hurts and bring them into consciousness, where they can be understood and integrated, rather than keep your body and your memories of the abuse trapped in fear, and undermining the present.

Having a conversation with your child after an episode of sudden, strong emotion is not about devaluing that emotion or diminishing your adult experience. Sometimes we have good reason to be upset or angry or frustrated or depressed. That's life for everyone. But it's possible to handle the ups and downs of life differently when your body and mind understand that every disappointment, encounter with an unhappy person, or potential love match is not a matter of life and death, as your current wiring insists it is.

When the child feels safe and the healthy adult part of you is fully in charge and aware on every level that the abuse is over, your fear-based reactions to life diminish, because your body's fight/flight system and brain finally calm down. It's not enough to simply tell yourself the abuse is over. Engaging the child part of yourself in the most caring, realistic way you can lets the child *experience* love and safety. And that seems to be the key to communicating with all the body/mind elements that can reinterpret the experience of abuse and free you from the sense that you are perpetually under threat.

The job of repairing and reparenting the child takes practice and persistence. Keep at it, and eventually all the intellectual understandings you have about your abuse will come into you through the experience of your child, and your knowing will become integrated with what the child's heart knows. This will allow you to expand into all your potential. You will truly be in charge of your life. Your past will no longer run you. And your emotions will no longer run *over* you.

Keep going.

7

ASSIGNING RESPONSIBILITY
What Belongs to the Abuser, and What Belongs to You?

Writing your story from both the adult's and the child's point of view may be the first time you've brought together the facts of what happened to you with the emotional truth of the child's experience. That's a powerful beginning. This process is teaching you to exist in total honesty, to build empathy for the child, and to believe in yourself.

Now I want to drill into the core truth of what happened to you: *It wasn't your fault. It was absolutely and unquestionably the fault of your abuser. It was a crime. It's against the law!*

I know I've been saying this since the first pages of this book. And I know that you know it intellectually and believe you can say those words to your child. But it was painful, and intensely fright-ening, for the child to be hurt, neglected, disdained, or belittled by the people who were supposed to provide safety and love. The child decided he or she was to blame, because any other explanation was too terrifying. Often the abuser reinforced that perception with words such as "Don't make me hit you again" or "You brought this on yourself."

The hurt child inside you still feels tremendously guilty and ashamed, both for having been abused and for "deserving it," and those feelings are etched in the body's hidden memories. At the same time, you may never have stepped back as an adult to examine the rationalizations you've probably been using for decades to let your abuser(s) off the hook.

So I want you to spend time now working with both your child and the healthy adult part of yourself to dismantle the familiar arguments about why the abuse was somehow okay, and why your smartest move is to forgive and forget so you can move on with your life. The pull to do so is especially strong at this point, because the work you've done so far has brought so much buried pain to the surface, and that often intensifies the desire to retreat into denial.

I want to emphasize: This is not the time to minimize what happened. This is the moment when you must strip away every excuse and rationalization and hold your abuser(s) accountable for what they did.

It's not easy to do this. My clients feel an instinctive urge to protect their "loved ones" or those in trusted positions (teachers, clergy members, coaches), even when they were the abusers. They also want to protect themselves. Initially, it's common to fear that one won't be believed, and will instead be shamed and blamed into staying silent. People hold on to the hope that if they don't talk about what happened, it'll just go away. And they believe that if they just understood what made their abusers act the way they did, everything would make more sense and they'd finally have some peace.

But what is there to understand? Let me repeat: Abusing children is morally wrong, legally wrong, spiritually wrong—it's every kind of wrong. No amount of good your abuser(s) did takes away from the crime. No gift or "treat" erases the punching or beating or sexual violation. No amount of fear your parents or guardian might have felt about confronting the abuser and getting you to safety makes up for the fact that they didn't protect you.

You can't bypass the pain and skip ahead to forgiveness. You must hold your abuser(s) responsible for damaging the innocent child you were. At your own pace, you will grow to have the courage to see what happened, speak your truth, and stand up for the child. The hard work you're doing in this book is making that possible.

At the same time, you must take responsibility for your part in this process: You are 100 percent responsible for your recovery. Though you are blameless for the abuse you experienced and it may not seem fair that you have to do this hard, painful work yourself, only you can rescue your child. Only you can provide the parenting that will allow the child to heal so you can repair your life. And if you don't step up to become the good parent your child never had, you will continue to subject the child to the blame, shame, neglect, and pain your abuser(s) inflicted on you. You must take responsibility for your child to end the cycle of abuse.

Doing this will mean learning to stop yourself in the midst of habitual thoughts and actions, and to insert two new players in the process: the good parent you are learning to be, and the child, whose presence will make it increasingly difficult to tell yourself damaging old stories or to hide out in the abuser(s)' version of the past. I know you probably feel pulled to protect your abuser(s) because it's what you've always done, but keep your photo of your child in view as you do the work of this chapter. Above all else, that is the person you need to protect now.

Use the words I'll teach you to fight back any time the embers of rationalization flare into warm feelings of understanding and forgiveness toward your abuser(s) and those who failed to protect you. Those feelings are both inappropriate and dangerous right now. Today, you must single-mindedly stand up for your child and fire-hose any sparks of "It wasn't a big deal" or "It was really my fault" with the arguments that follow. Do it until it's boring. Until it's second nature. Until the rationalizations feel wrong in your mind and mouth.

I know you can, and you *must*.

LET'S TALK ABOUT RESPONSIBILITY NOT BLAME

What would your story, or any of the stories you've seen so far in this book, look like as a police or news report?

- "The adult perpetrator beat the five-year-old child with belt buckles, wire hangers, brooms, cable wire."
- "The perpetrator subjected the child to taunts and name-calling, continually using labels such as 'stupid,' 'whore,' 'worthless,' 'piece of shit.'"
- "The perpetrator brandished a gun and held it at the head of his spouse as the children watched."
- "The adult perpetrator fondled the genitals of the seven-year-old child and left a four-year-old alone with a sexual predator. The adults in the household never followed up on the twelve-year-old's complaints that he was being molested."
- "The child was subjected to controlling behavior and emotional abuse repeatedly for years."
- "The perpetrator left the six-year-old child to shop, cook meals, and care for himself while the perpetrator brought drug-using friends into the home and shot up with them."

It's abundantly clear, when you strip your story to its essence—what an abuser did to the child you were—that we're looking at criminal behavior. It's against the law to treat children with this kind of cruelty, neglect, and abuse.

If you, as an adult, witnessed a child being subjected to this kind of treatment, you'd intervene. You would feel morally obligated to report the crime. Look at the small, innocent child in the photo you carry with you and speak to every day. Imagine the events of that child's story put into the cool, objective language of a police report, the language of perpetrators and victims. How could anyone treat a child that way? The abuse was a crime. Someone should have reported it.

Who was your abuser? Was it a parent? Sibling? Cousin? Teacher? The parent of a friend? Neighbor? Coach? Priest? Only you can answer this question. Take a moment. Name the abuser(s) in your mind. Child abuse is a crime, no matter who committed it.

I know your brain knows this. You've written your story. You've named names. Yet even after all that, nearly everyone I work with tells me, "I don't want to heap blame on them. That was a long time ago. They didn't know what they were doing/They're different now/ They did the best they could."

I've thought a lot about why no one wants to use the word "blame" in talking about the past, and I have a hunch that the reason might be embedded in the word itself. "Blame" has the same root as the word "blaspheme": "blasphemos." It's a Greek word that means "evil-speaking." And I think people worry about blaming their parents and abusers for the abuse because it feels like blasphemy, "speaking evil" about sacred things. We tend to hold parents and trusted guardians sacred, no matter what they've done.

So let's take blame out of the equation entirely. Instead, let's talk about assigning responsibility. Assigning responsibility isn't an emotional thing. It's simple and rational. It allows you to look at what happened and ask: "Whose job was it to take care of the child in the house? Who was responsible? Did the people in my life live up to their responsibilities?"

The answer is not a mystery, and it's not complicated. It's the adult's job to care for the little person. Doing that job well, or even minimally, requires attention and a willingness to put the needs of someone vulnerable ahead of the adult's—no matter how inconvenient that may be. The child's welfare comes first. That means finding a way to feed the baby or child when he or she is hungry, keeping the child safe from harm, and giving this boy or girl shelter, education, and love. Parents are responsible too for doing their best to equip the child emotionally for navigating the world as a free, independent adult, something that starts with ensuring that the child has a strong sense of self, a sense of being valued and valuable.

No parent is perfect, and all parents will look back and see where they've fallen short. But at the barest minimum, the parent is responsible for protecting the child from harm.

In looking back at the details of what happened to the child you were, ask: "Did the adults do the job they were supposed to?" We're not asking, "Would they have done better if things were different for them?" or "Did they mean to do better?" We're asking: "Did they live up to their responsibilities?"

If you were abused, the answer is no. And the abuser(s) alone are responsible for the harm they caused you and the crimes they committed.

I want to remind you of one other thing, which is crucial: You may think the abuse is forgivable because it was "a long time ago," but your child has never stopped experiencing it. It's a part of him or her, locked inside in sensations so vivid they can feel at any moment as though the abuse is happening right now. The adult part of you has the power to show your child that he or she is safe now, protected from the abuser(s) who still loom so large. Showing the child the abuse has stopped means holding abusers accountable.

"YES, BUT . . ."

Despite all that, I know you'd probably like to turn the black-and-white realities of your abuse into shades of gray and explain away what was done to you. It blunts the pain to let yourself believe the abuse was some kind of accident, and that the abuser(s) really didn't mean to hurt you and wouldn't have done it except for some extenuating circumstance. But I will not allow you to let the perpetrator(s) off the hook for what they did. I will not let you explain away your child's trauma, or say it wasn't that big a deal. When you do that, you abandon the child, who is beginning to trust you, and throw that child back into all his or her pain. You give yourself over to the abuser(s) when you make excuses for them.

For every person you protect, your inner child takes on that much more guilt, shame, and blame. As long as you continue to make excuses for the abuser(s), you will never be whole. You'll continue to split yourself between their lies and the truth. And you know how *that's* turned out so far. Living their lies is ruining your life. That's how this works.

You cause your child intense suffering when you excuse your abuser(s) by using phrases such as those that follow. They're poison. Get them out of your vocabulary and fight for your child by acknowledging the truth.

Your child will feel stronger and safer every time you stand up for him or her instead of making excuses for the people who abused you.

LET'S TAKE APART THE WAY YOU EXCUSE THE ABUSERS

- THEY DID THE BEST THEY COULD UNDER THE CIRCUMSTANCES. Guess what? The best they could was not good enough! If you had a job and you were doing the best you could but you were not doing what was required of you—and, in fact, you committed a crime at work—you would be fired. "The best you could do" would not hold up as being nearly good enough. You'd fail at your job, just as your abuser(s) failed at theirs. That's the fact. The truth is not that they "did their best" but that they *failed to protect and nurture you*. And the result was abuse.

"They did the best they could under the circumstances" is a particularly tricky set of words for people in twelve-step programs because they are often used in the process of releasing resentments, forgiving those who have done harm, and moving on from the past. That's not appropriate here, at least not right now. Before we can talk about forgiveness, we have to understand exactly what was done and be very clear, especially for the child's sake, about who was responsible for the abuse.

I cannot let you forgive anyone until you know exactly what you are forgiving. Waving a wand that says "You did your best; I forgive you" is a spiritual bypass, and a betrayal and abandonment of your child. It's meaningless. You cannot forgive your abuser(s)—if you decide to do that—until you grow the courage to see exactly what happened, understand the effects of what your abuser(s) did to you and the child, hold the abuser(s) accountable, and speak your truth to them. *Then* you can forgive.

"They did their best" doesn't cut it. They harmed and failed to protect you. The best they could do was to allow an innocent child to be abused.

- THEY WERE UNDER STRESS/ALCOHOLIC/DEPRESSED. Parents and caregivers are not supposed to neglect, berate, beat, or rape children—their own or anyone else's—no matter what the circumstances. Can you imagine a guidebook titled *How to Be a Good Parent* that included the advice: "If you're depressed, drunk, or angry, you are excused from the laws of the land, and may physically, emotionally, or sexually abuse your children at will. It's a good way to let off a little steam"? Your caregivers were responsible for seeking treatment for their conditions and addictions so they could help you thrive. If they needed help coping, their job was to get it. If they needed medication or counseling or parenting help, their responsibility was to seek it out. *That* was their job, no matter what. You were not born to be the designated punching bag and caretaker.

The beautiful child in your photo deserved to be loved, protected, and cared for.

- THEY HAD IT HARD TOO. A tough life is not an excuse. We're talking about perpetrating a crime because life is difficult. Most people manage to face even the most grueling challenges without robbing a bank, pulling out a gun, or beating up their kids. A hard day at work is no excuse for terrorizing, neglecting, or otherwise abusing an innocent child. There is *no* excuse for that.

- THEY DIDN'T KNOW ANY BETTER. The truth is, abusers *hide* abuse. That is, they are aware enough to know what they're doing is wrong and will get them into trouble. Far from being "innocent" in any way, abusers believe they can get away with crimes of abuse. They believe they can keep the abuse undetectable and that they can do anything they like when they're not in public. They believe the laws don't apply to them. They believe there won't be any witnesses. They believe children are too weak to tell the truth. They believe even if a child did tell the truth, no adult would believe that child. They know how powerful they are, and they choose to use that power to abuse.

- THAT'S THE WAY PEOPLE DISCIPLINED KIDS BACK THEN. Steven held on tightly to this rationalization after he'd told his story the first few times. Sure his parents had beaten him and washed his mouth out with soap, but "That was the way it was in those days," he repeatedly argued. "They considered it appropriate discipline, and that's how they were taught. It wasn't their fault. Everybody did that."

  All that may be true, I told him, but it doesn't change what happened to that kid, or how the kid is suffering now because of what happened to him. You can't minimize what they did to you regardless of their intention. The abuse was real. It was extremely destructive, with lifelong consequences. What happened to the child from the child's perspective was not okay—abusing a child never is, and never has been. "Everybody" did not brutalize and terrorize their children. And even if they had, every abuser would have known that what they were doing was destroying the soul of the child. A child's eyes don't lie. No one can pretend away that pain. Abusers see it, and they ignore it. They want the gratification of the abuse more than they want to protect their own precious children.

- THEY WERE TOO AFRAID TO PROTECT ME. It's all too common for one parent to keep quiet about the abuse perpetrated by the other parent, to keep children in an abusive situation, or to look the other way and pretend the abuse is not going on. That parent may even punish the child for seeking his or her comfort and protection. The quiet parent enables the abuse to continue, and in doing so, that parent is guilty of acting as an accessory, an accomplice, and an enabler of this crime. Especially in dangerous and threatening situations, the non-abusive parent's most important job is to take the children to safety. Decent parents call on every bit of courage they have to get themselves and their kids away from abusers. Fear is not an excuse. "Mom had no skills and needed to stay with Dad to survive" is not an excuse. Adults have choices. There are *always* options. A parent who stays in an abusive situation is saying, "If I have to let my child be beaten, raped, and emotionally abused to keep a roof over my head, that's the price the kid will have to pay." Fear and danger are reasons to remove a child from peril, not reasons to stay.

It is not little children's job to worry over the safety of a mother who keeps them in an abusive situation. They are not responsible for her, and in letting them take that responsibility, she is robbing them of their innocence, their freedom, their childhood. They were supposed to be protected, not sacrificed to abuse because of a parent's fear.

If you see your mother or any other silent family member as a victim, you allow the child—the weakest one of all—to carry the weight alone, for everyone. This is not how things should ever be.

- THE NON-PROTECTIVE PARENT DIDN'T KNOW WHAT WAS GOING ON. I don't buy for a second that a parent would not know if his or her child were being abused, even if the child didn't or couldn't say a word. Have you ever cared for a pet? It's not hard to tell when an animal isn't feeling well—its eating patterns change, and it might suddenly behave differently, becoming more aggressive or seeking out an unusual corner to sleep. If I can tell when something's wrong with my cat, Scarlett, you can bet that I—or any adult—could pick up that something is wrong when a child is being abused. A parent's job is to hear and see the child, notice changes—and find out what's going on.

Mothers often say "I have eyes in the back of my head,"

and perhaps they do when it comes to catching a child breaking a rule or stealing a cookie. But I often wonder where those eyes are when their children are being abused. I have talked in depth with parents who claim they didn't notice any changes in their children and didn't know abuse was taking place. I find most of them eventually admit they had a feeling something was wrong, but they chose to dismiss the signs and ignore their intuition.

We must destroy the myth that parents deserve our forgiveness when they claim they didn't know what was going on in their own homes. We all know what a parent should do, because it's shockingly easy. When a parent notices a change in a child's behavior, he or she investigates. And when the parent discovers evidence of child abuse, the parent calls the police. It's that simple. The parent picks up the phone and makes a call. The parent presses charges. The parent follows through. That's it. That's how parents should behave.

There's not a bit of confusion about this in the legal system. If the adults in a family don't protect the child and a social worker goes into that home and discovers physical or sexual abuse, the child is taken away, even if one parent claims he or she didn't know it was happening. The environment is deemed unsafe for the child to remain in because *no one was protecting the child*.

When parents pay attention and intervene early, they can lessen the impact of the abuse on the child. The intervention shows their kids they are protected, someone is watching out for them, and someone cares enough to make sure the abuser *never* gets another chance. That's absolutely crucial to the child's emotional recovery. The more the parent denies the abuse, the more the child suffers because of it. The more we live the lie, the worse our lives get.

The parent who "did not know" should have known. No excuses.

- THE ABUSER HAD SO MUCH POWER, NO ONE COULD COMPLAIN. Who needs protection more—the powerful abuser or the innocent child? Anyone who does not try to stop an abuser becomes complicit in the abuse, and in any future abuse that occurs. I remember the story of a man who, as a child, was sexually abused by his grandfather. When the grandfather died, the local newspaper published an article that described the grandfather as a great man in the community. At his funeral, family and friends gathered to celebrate the grandfather's wonderful life. And in talking to each other, they learned that the grandfather had abused several members of the family over a long period. No one had spoken up about their abuse.

Why? They had thought, mistakenly, that they were the grandfather's only victims. They had been afraid no one would believe this "wonderful" man had abused them. They had been afraid the rest of the family, as well as the community, would blame them for selfishly trying to stain the reputation of this "great" man.

And as a result, the grandfather had been free to abuse family members from one generation to the next. The family chose silence, and in silence they suffered.

GOOD DEEDS DO NOT ERASE THE TRUTH

There's one more category of "protect the abuser" rationalizations I'd like to focus on at slightly greater length. My clients and I call it the mindfuck. It involves abusers who try to "make up" for the abuse with gifts, never taking responsibility for the damage they've caused and often dealing out "good" treatment with one hand and abuse with the other. Especially when the gifts are significant, it's easy to rationalize that it's better to just forget the abuse and take advantage of "the good stuff."

Don't do it. Nothing bought with the suffering of your child, who *still* suffers and fears the abuser, is a gift. It may be a bribe, but it's not an act of kindness. It's a mindfuck, designed to keep you confused and prevent you from standing up for the child.

I once treated a woman whose stepfather sexually abused her every night from the time she was four years old. She remembered what had happened. Yet when she came to me, she protected him. She knew the abuse was wrong and that it had affected her life in ways that were not good for her. Her desperation drove her to therapy, but she continued to rationalize the abuse, saying he had saved her and her mother from a life of poverty, sent her to college and to Europe, and provided her with a beautiful home. Her abuser, she told me, was kind, generous, and fatherly.

But no matter what else he had done in her life, he had sexually abused her, traumatized her, and hurt her. And the lasting damage was incalculable. She felt worthless and suicidal, incapable of happiness or closeness. *That* was the stepfather's lasting "gift" to her: a lifetime of suffering.

The mindfuck works because the good deeds of an abuser confuse children, who have difficulty reconciling good and evil in one person. Abusers take advantage of this to keep their victims off balance. And everyone in the chain of abuse—the abuser, the abused child, and even the other family members—uses these good deeds not just to excuse criminal behavior but to cover it up, to make it disappear, to bury the abuse deep in the shadows. The more you build up the good deeds, the easier it is to pretend the abuse is inconsequential and push it away.

My client and her family tried to point to the stepfather's financial support as evidence that he had "righted" his wrong. But an abuser can't erase his or her crimes and their searing impact with money. Parents can't pay to molest a child, or pay their victims to forget. Abusers can't buy off a judge to let them commit crimes. And you can't overlook the devastation abusers caused in your life when they take out the checkbook to pay for college or cars or trips. None of that does anything to diminish the pain you have carried with you into adulthood. Money can't change the truth. Money can't buy peace or freedom for the suffering child inside you.

Abuse murders a child's soul. It demolishes innocence. You could have lived a free and happy life, but your abuser(s) took that possibility away from you. When they think they can get away with it, guilt-free, they don't understand. They don't get that you're paying for their abuse every day of your life, and it doesn't go away because they've "bought" you college, a fancy car, or a foreign country. You carry the effects of that abuse with you. They pay with a credit card; you pay with your life.

LET'S DISMANTLE THE WAYS YOU BLAME YOURSELF

There's a second particularly damaging variety of rationalizations for the abusers' behavior, arguments that have often been planted and fed by the abusers themselves. These are the rationalizations that say the child "caused" the abuse. Abuse victims use this toxic reasoning to blame themselves instead of putting responsibility for the abuse on the abusers, where it belongs. (I notice that the word "blame" suddenly stops being an issue for my clients when they're directing it toward themselves instead of their parents.)

These rationalizations are insidious statements that the child inside you is all too ready to believe. So before I list them, let me emphasize: The only person at fault for the abuse is the perpetrator. *All* responsibility for it lies with the adult. The abuse was *not* the fault of the child you were. That child was in no way responsible for any of the abuser's crimes. *The child was innocent.*

If you find yourself falling back on statements like the ones that follow to minimize the abuse you faced, or to explain it away, *stop*. Pull out your photo and look at your child's face and at his or her small body. You may well think that as a child you were mature beyond your years and somehow complicit in the abuse. Many of my clients think they were six going on twenty-six when they were abused. But the fact is, an eight-year-old or a twelve-year-old is a *child* who needs to be taught, nurtured, and protected, not exploited and abused. I can't say this often enough: The child was innocent. You were innocent. You bear no responsibility for what happened.

If you think you deserve the abuse you suffered, then look at everyone you see in this book, and every child you know and read about who was abused, and tell them they deserved it too. It's all or nothing. We're all guilty of provoking our parents, or we're not.

You are not to blame for your abuse. Don't let yourself say or believe anything that suggests you "brought the abuse on yourself" for reasons like those that follow. You have a choice now. Let the healthy adult part of you notice whenever you fall into the habit of blaming the child for what happened. Then shield the child from these toxic beliefs. Look at the photo you carry and reassure the child. Say: "I love you, and I'm sorry for what happened to you. It was not your fault. You deserved better. You're safe now. I'm here to protect you."

- I WAS A REBEL/A PROBLEM CHILD/A KID WHO NEVER OBEYED. Children are not miniature adults. They are young, developing individuals who learn limits, boundaries, and behavior—everything they know—from the people who care for them. A child does not deserve abuse for any reason, and labeling a child rebellious, "a problem," or disobedient does not justify mistreatment. Kids don't act out for no reason. They do it because that's what they see their parents doing or in response to the fears they face in their households or because they're wired for activity but born into homes where they're expected to be still and silent— and a million other reasons that have nothing to do with "being a bad seed" or "deserving" abuse. If your five-year-old got hyperactive in the supermarket or squirmy at church, would you beat him or her with a belt or pummel that child with hateful verbal abuse? I didn't think so.

- I WAS A TROUBLEMAKER AND THEY DIDN'T KNOW WHAT TO DO WITH ME. What's a troublemaker? A kid who screams when his mom or sibling is being beaten? A child who runs away from home to escape abuse? A little boy or girl who does anything he or she can to get someone to pay attention so they'll see what's happening at home?

  Children don't bring abuse on themselves. Abuse is a decision made by an adult to harm a child. The labels an abuser puts on a child are self-serving. Don't accept the family labels or the myth that you were the reason your abuser(s) hurt you. They were the big people, and you were the small one in need of protection.

- "I WAS SEXUALLY PROVOCATIVE." "I ENJOYED THE SEX." "I WANTED IT." The rules are clear and sane in our culture: Adults do not have sex with children or allow children to be used sexually by others. The adult's job is to teach children how to keep themselves safe from sexual exploitation and to protect their bodies.

The truth is, children have sexual feelings. Every client I have, male or female, who was sexually abused as a child will tell me, "Even when I was tiny, I remember having sexual feelings. Sex felt good. I wanted more." They say this with guilt, and think those natural sensations—the result of their bodies doing what they were designed to do—are the reason they were singled out for abuse. *But children's sexual feelings do not make them culpable in their abuse.*

Children learn early that certain kinds of touching feel good to them. But it's the parents' or caretakers' job to teach the child what to do with that sexual energy. Good parents don't capitalize on their children's inherent sexuality; they redirect it. The good parent says, "Go put your clothes on in public" and "That is your private place. Only you can touch it." That's how children learn boundaries, and how to stay safe.

A child who does not receive that kind of training is vulnerable to abuse and manipulation far into adulthood. He or she doesn't learn to say "no" or "stop" or "I don't want to." And when that child learns the abuser's "normal" violates a strong social taboo, the sense of shame is overpowering. Victims feel incredibly guilty because they were coerced into doing something wrong, and their bodies felt pleasure. They blame themselves for their own violation. Now sex and intimacy are linked in the victims' core with guilt, exploitation, pain, and "dirtiness." They may simply withdraw from intimate adult relationships because that vital realm feels so dangerous to them and produces such feelings of fear and shame. Or they may be drawn to situations that feel dangerously familiar, with a power imbalance like the one they faced during the abuse.

Did the child agree to all this? Want it? Understand the damage? Ask to be robbed of easy adult intimacy and the ability to trust a partner sexually when it was safe and appropriate to? Did the child ask to feel violated, dirty, and ashamed for the rest of his or her life?

That child was four or eight or twelve years old. The child did not "ask for it" or "provoke" the abuse. The child was used, and that little boy or girl's experience of sexual pleasure was twisted, tainted, and used against him or her. What a terrible thing to do to a child.

ABUSE IS A POISON

Abuse is an act of hostility. The abuser may try to make the abuse look like an act of love—"I only did it to keep you from getting too wild" or "What's wrong with a mother being close to her son?"—but those lies and blame and rationalizations and bribes are poisonous. And if you keep swallowing the lies and letting the abuser off the hook, you will poison your child, and you will start to die inside. This kind of poison kills many parts of ourselves—our souls, our health, our identities— and leaves us too weak to take control of our own lives.

You must not say: "A little abuse was okay" or "A little abuse didn't hurt me" or "They did their best, so it's okay" or "I brought it on myself."

Do not swallow the poison. Do not let your child swallow a single drop. You can protect your child now. You must.

WHAT *ARE* YOU RESPONSIBLE FOR? YOUR RECOVERY.

Protecting your child from the poison of self-blame and minimizing the past is one of your vital jobs as a parent. Please treat it as a sacred trust. And please continue to protect and nurture your child in every way, every day. That is your responsibility, and you *are* on the hook 100 percent for that crucial job. You must be unconditionally on the child's side, loving, supporting, and caring for that little girl or boy.

Unconditional love says: "I'm going to love you no matter what happens, no matter what you do, no matter how you feel, no matter what you say. I'm going to listen to you and be here for you no matter how much you try to push me away." That is what your child deserves from you.

I've emphasized repeatedly that when a child is born, the big person is responsible for the little person. The parent's job is to guide the physical, emotional, social, and spiritual development of the child, to tend that child. Doing this for the child inside you—consistently, lovingly, responsibly—is what will heal both of you. You have got to show up for your child the way your parents never showed up for you. And you have to *keep* showing up, being brave, drawing the child out, and putting the child first.

Your little boy or little girl's needs *have* to come before anything else. That didn't happen for you when you were growing up, and it's going to take work to break your old habits of neglect and ignoring the child. But I believe you can. The child is alive inside you. And as you learn to listen to your child, you will grow as a parent and create a new, loving foundation for your life.

- Keep checking in with your child morning and night.
- Keep examining strong feelings by asking the child when he or she first remembers experiencing them.
- When you hear yourself starting to let your abuser(s) off the hook, or taking the blame for what happened to you, stop and remind the child that he or she is innocent, and what happened was wrong.
- If the child needs a hug, give one to him or her.

Sometimes what the child wants to be told is so simple: "I'm here. I heard you. I love you." Honor and protect your child. Every day.

FIND THE COURAGE TO HEAL

In the decades I have worked with adults who were abused as children, I have seen many people heal and recover their lives. They've done it by summoning the courage to keep facing the truth of their abuse, even when they were afraid.

Half measures won't do. You must stop taking blame for what

happened to you. Doing so only continues the abuse begun so long ago. It's your job, today, to protect your child and to lift the crushing burden of responsibility for the abuse from his or her narrow shoulders.

Practice doing this concretely, and in the safety of your notebook, by completing the following exercises.

ASSIGNMENT 1: Write Letters to the Abuser(s)

The letters you'll write now are not intended to be read by anyone other than you. It is not time to confront your perpetrators. Use these letters to get clarity about your abuser(s), how the abuse affected you, and who was responsible for the harm that was done to you.

First, write to your aggressor or most abusive parent or family member, using this familiar template.

Name_____:

When you did _____ to me,
it made me feel _____.
How dare you do _____ to me.
Your job was to love and take care of me, not to hurt me.

And then continue to write whatever you feel.

Example:

Dad:

When you beat me with that board you had drilled holes in so it would move faster and hurt that much more, it made me feel humiliated, terrified, and helpless. I felt like I was going to die, and you broke my spirit.

How dare you beat me, humiliate me, terrify me, and break my spirit!

I was your innocent child, and your job was to love me. How dare you make me suffer instead!

Write letters to cover each two-year period you were abused—for example, from ages six to eight, eight to ten, then ten to twelve, twelve to fourteen, and so on.

ASSIGNMENT 2: Write Letters to Those Who Kept Silent

Write a letter to someone who kept silent, such as a parent, sibling, or other family member. Tell that non-protector what happened to you, and that he or she should have known and should have done something to stop the abuse. Use words like "You failed to protect me."

You may write more than one letter here. There may be many people who knew and kept silent. You may write letters to your stepparents, grandparents, brothers, sisters, aunts, uncles, and cousins.

Please do this in a safe place. This exercise will bring up many intense emotions. If you feel emotionally unsafe at any time during these writings, please stop and seek help and support. Again, it's important to recognize you are in the here and now. You are safe and free from danger. You are the adult standing up for and protecting the child inside you.

ASSIGNMENT 3: Read Your Letters Aloud

You may repeat this exercise in the future. But for now, to bring this step to a close, please read these letters aloud. In a private space, stand up and picture the people the letters were meant for, and direct your words to them. You are safe. Read with all the emotion you feel. Get angry, get loud, and cry. You might want to record yourself as you read and listen later, paying attention to what you hear then.

Remember to protect yourself and your child by seeking support if you need it.

ASSIGNMENT 4: Write a Letter to Your Child

Imagine you are visiting your child, who is alone and suffering after one of the instances of abuse you wrote about. Tell the child he or she is not to blame. Say the words the child most needs to hear: "You are not responsible for what happened to you. Your abuser(s) did a bad thing, but you did nothing wrong. You are innocent. You are safe now, and I will protect you. I love you."

Pull out your photo of the child and read your letter aloud to him or her. Use whatever soothing techniques make the child feel safe, loved, and protected.

ASSIGNMENT 5: Communicate With the Child Using Right Hand/Left Hand

This is difficult work. Check in with the child to find out how he or she is doing. Don't forget to respond to what the child tells you.

ASSIGNMENT 6: Revisit Your Story

If any of this work brings up details you'd like to add to your story, or if you notice language in your story that minimizes the abuser(s)' role, go back and make revisions.

8

PROTECT THE CHILD NOW
With a Ninety-Day Break
From Your Abusers

You've done a lot of writing to this point. Now I'd like you to step out of the notebook and take a bold, direct action to honor and protect your child. It won't be comfortable, but being 100 percent responsible for your recovery means giving your child what he or she needs the most in this moment. And what the child needs above all is an atmosphere of complete safety.

You cannot heal, and your child will not feel protected, as long as you are enmeshed in your old ways of being within the circle of abuse. So for ninety days, I'd like you to eliminate all contact with anyone who was party to the abuse, either silently or actively. This includes parents, caretakers, family members, and any person who participated in the abuse or failed to keep you safe. I'd also like you to take a break from seeing anyone who tries to pull you back into the old family system of denial and rationalizing—even if they're siblings who also faced abuse under the same roof. No one really understands how your abuse affected you and what your experience was like, even if the same thing happened to them. You need space to process your experience on your own. *You need physical distance to get emotional clarity.*

I want you to tell all these people what you're going to do, and then honor your commitment to yourself and your child by holding firm for these ninety days of separation.

In doing this, you'll be making a loud, clear statement to your inner child: "The past is over. This is a new beginning, a chance to do the work that will bring lasting change."

I know I'm asking a lot. No one wants to do this, and some of the greatest resistance I see in clients comes up when I ask them to take this three-month break. But it's the only way to get the time and perspective you need to recover. Any time you're pulled into old family dynamics, your old ways of being cloud your vision. Those emotional habits and patterns trap you in the past, paralyzing you and preventing you from breaking away, taking control, and moving forward. But from the moment you tell your abuser(s) and the people who didn't protect you that you intend to take this hiatus, you'll gain invaluable insights into the workings of the relationship you have with them. The emotional atmosphere you've been living in will become visible to you, and you'll be able to stand apart from it and decide, for the first time, how you want things to be.

"YOU WANT ME TO DO *WHAT*?"

Rose had been working diligently to be a good parent to her little girl, steadily building her relationship with the child inside her. As she kept the right-hand/left-hand conversation going, she was remembering more pieces of her past. "I was abused 365 days a year for many years," she told me, almost surprised, "and that daily abuse is something I didn't really think about until I started this process."

The memories that were surfacing had unleashed "a tornado of feelings," she added—great sadness for her child, and intense anger. She was willing to work with all of that, she said, and to do anything that could help her little girl.

But when I suggested it was time to spend three months focused only on her healing, with no contact with her family, she balked. Like many of my clients, she had maintained close ties to her abusive and non-protective family members, pretending nothing had changed inside her. We went round and round for weeks, as she argued that she couldn't possibly take a break from them even for ninety days, because her mother, who was still living with her abusive father, needed her. "I call my mom every day," she told me. "What is she going to do if I'm not there?"

I didn't understand her culture, she said. "I'm Latin, and coming from that background, you never turn your back on your parents."

It's a common worry that by breaking contact, you will be abandoning your family, I told her, even though ninety days falls far short of "forever." In truth, this break is less about turning away from the family than turning toward yourself so you can focus on your recovery. As we continue, it's vital to examine yourself fully and honestly, and you can't do it while you're mired in the patterns of the past. The people who truly love you and want the best for you won't object to your taking time to heal.

Rose was terrified of telling her family she needed this time to reflect and do her inner work, and she didn't think it was necessary, but she began to realize that even though she had moved out from under her parents' roof years ago, she was still emotionally there, doing whatever they asked, cringing away from the verbal abuse her father still heaped on her. They still had control.

What was keeping her so enmeshed? Interestingly enough, it was her child's fears. After all the hurt the abusers and non-protectors have inflicted, the child inside can only see one thing worse than the abuse—the possibility the abusers will leave. The adult Rose talked about not wanting to abandon family, but her child's underlying fear was that this break would be an opportunity for *them* to do the abandoning. The child's concern was: "What if they don't want me back?"

It took time and courage, and many conversations with her child, but finally Rose decided she had to act. Each time she took her child into her parents' company, she was sending her back into the war zone, and keeping alive all the terror of the past. And as a loving parent, she couldn't keep pretending away the damage. She reassured Little Rose that they'd take care of each other over the three-month stretch—and at last, she committed to making the break.

It was near the end of the year, and Rose's three-month hiatus would include Christmas and New Year's, which had always been flashpoint family holidays. She expected fireworks when she announced she would not be attending, but she held on to her resolve. She wanted to heal more than she wanted to keep the peace.

FIGURING OUT WHAT TO SAY

We worked on what she would tell her parents, and how she would say it. There's no need to walk into a tough conversation like this cold, and it makes sense to write out your message and practice reading it aloud until you feel comfortable.

"Things will go the most smoothly if you keep things simple," I told her. "Your job is to announce your decision, not to go into lengthy explanations, justifications, or defenses. Just say something short and honest, like this:

"Mom and Dad, I'm doing some deep work on myself right now and I need to have some time alone. I won't be talking to you or keeping in contact for the next three months. This is important to me, and I'll really appreciate your giving me the time and space that I'm requesting to do this work.

"I will call you in three months and I'll let you know what's going on. If there's an emergency, of course let me know. Thank you for respecting my wishes. We'll talk in three months."

I know this may be the first time you've ever stood up for yourself and made a direct request of your parents that goes against their expectations and "the way it's always been." I know how scary it can be to say, "This is what I want." But announcing your decision to take this time away from your family will make a huge difference to your sense of personal power and self-respect. By putting the child's healing and well-being ahead of your fear, you are claiming your adulthood and growing into the good parent your child has always deserved.

DEALING WITH THE RESPONSES

I suggest that you have this conversation by phone so that if you want or need to, you can write out what you want to say and read it to the abuser(s). It's a good way to stay on track if you feel nervous or tongue-tied. A phone call has another great advantage: You can control when the conversation ends.

Your abuser(s) will no doubt have questions, comments, and, if they're like so many abusive parents, emotional attacks. Don't be drawn into a discussion or a defense of what you've decided to do. Instead, be prepared with a clear response that acknowledges what they've said.

You can say things such as:

- I really need to do this to take care of myself.
- I understand, however I need you to respect my decision.
- I'm sorry you feel that way, but that's what I'm going to do.
- I understand, but this is about me taking care of myself.
- I understand, but that's what I'm going to do.
- Mom, I love you. I'll talk to you in three months.

- I'm not punishing you; I'm working on myself. Thanks for respecting my decision.
- I will get back to you in three months, and we'll talk then.

Pick one or two responses, and stick to them. Repeat them like a broken record. This isn't a negotiation or argument—it takes two engaged parties to have either of those, and you are not engaging. You're making your announcement and ending the conversation.

If verbal abuse starts coming your way, immediately protect your child by interrupting and saying, "I have to stop you. I'll talk to you in three months. I'm hanging up now." Then do it.

It will feel strange to do this. You may feel incredibly guilty. But remember the guilt is an old habit. You're harming no one by taking this time for yourself. The truth is you're taking a giant step toward taking care of yourself for once, and doing what's best for you. Remember you have a right to take this time and space to work through the abuse they perpetrated. You have to claim this right for yourself. Every time you do, you're respecting and protecting yourself and your child, and carving out a safe, sane place for yourself in the world.

In case you're worried, I've found that even though people frequently tell me they're sure this break will kill their parents, no parents have ever died because an adult child took a three-month break from contact.

You have the strength to do this, and it will have to come from you—your abuser(s) and non-protectors(s) are focused on themselves, and the only person who will put your child first is you. Push through the guilt and fear. If you don't, you'll always be stopped by yourself and the people who hurt you.

YOU'LL LEARN FROM THE WAY THEY RESPOND

Rose was nervous about calling her parents, and she gave herself extra support by bookending the conversation, telling her OA sponsor what she was going to do and arranging to touch base with her once she'd made the call. You can do this with a friend, sponsor, or therapist, and I suggest you do. You can also practice with them beforehand if you're feeling shaky.

"I really anguished about this," Rose reported after she'd announced her plan. "It's the holidays. I knew my mom would have a heart attack. But I made the call. I said, 'My therapist said I will not be talking to you or seeing you or having any contact with the family, not even my godson, for ninety days.' I was shaking; it was so hard. My mom never liked you, and she *really* doesn't like you now," Rose told me with a smile, "but her response made me see how right I was to do this. Mom said, 'I feel like you just stabbed me in the stomach and I have blood all over me.'

"All of a sudden I could see that's what I was doing—cutting the umbilical cord. I'm thirty-five years old and my mom was having this reaction like I was killing her, just because I was taking a ninety-day break. No wonder I never felt like an independent adult. I had never seen the bond between us in that way."

Loving parents want what's best for their children, and while they might chafe, they respect their kids' boundaries. A good parent would say, "I'll miss you, but do what you have to do. Take your time. I can see how important this is to you." But most abusers and non-protectors make everything about themselves, as Rose's mother did. That's why it's so important to stop waiting for them to change, and to take steps to empower and heal yourself now.

The rewards of doing so are great. For Brad, who grew up under the controlling thumb of an abusive preacher father, announcing his three-month break from contact showed him a new side of the man he'd always feared.

"When I called to say I was going to take time away from him, it was a weird emotional thing for me," Brad said. "I saw my father go from being a big, scary monster to a little boy. I could hardly process it.

He had been told by *me* what I wanted. And he didn't know what to do. I was finally able to see that the emperor has no clothes. The minute I started setting boundaries, I knew I could finally be in charge of my life. I told him, 'I love you—you're my father—but I'm not close to you. If someone needs help in an emergency, let me know, but I'm taking some time for myself now. Please don't contact me.'

"I thought beforehand that I'd never be able to do it, but I survived, and it was one of the most liberating things I've ever done."

YOU WILL BE THE ONE WHO CHANGES

Sometimes people resist giving themselves this three-month span to work on themselves because, they tell me, "I didn't talk to my parents for two years once, and nothing changed." But taking this break is not about waiting for a miracle to turn your abuser(s) into kind, enlightened beings. It's about making space that's clear of their influence so *you* can change. You walk into this time as a different person than you're used to being, because from the moment you announce you want these three months for yourself, *you're* the one who's setting the limits and saying what you will and won't allow in your life.

You'll get plenty of practice enforcing your new boundaries as you manage your family's resistance to your wishes.

Jennifer remembered that her relationships with family members "became really interesting" when she took a break from contact with her abusive mother. "I heard from everyone, especially my brother and sister," she told me. "Everyone likes to keep things the way they are, and when someone like me comes along messing with the way it's always been, no one's happy. They just couldn't understand why I wasn't coming to Mom's house for her birthday. They didn't get it."

You job isn't to explain. Just pick an answer such as "I'm doing some work on myself and I need this time," and keep repeating it. This kind of exchange gets boring after a while, and your questioners may get tired of trying to provoke you to say something else. If they become critical, fall back on those handy neutral responses—"I'm sorry you feel that way" or "I understand"—and leave it at that.

And if you've asked someone not to call you but they don't respect the boundary, just say, "I asked you not to call. Please, no contact," and hang up. Make it your policy to delete texts and e-mails from those you've asked not to contact you. Don't even open them. File them in the trash.

Every time you do this, you're strengthening a muscle that will keep you safe as you go more deeply into this work. It's the part of you that says what it means and means what it says.

WHEN YOU CAN SEE THE PATTERNS, YOU CAN HEAL THEM

The clarity that can come from taking a break and being free from contact with the abuser and your dysfunctional, in-denial family can be startling. Jennifer found that after a couple of months away from her mom, she couldn't see her in quite the same way anymore. "I had always taken care of her, and I called her every day, because if I didn't she'd be upset," she told me. "I was the jokester, the one who dyed her hair and cheered her up. We said we were best friends! But when I wasn't around her all the time, I began to notice that everyone was always afraid to make her angry—that's what some of those calls from my siblings were really about. We were scared of her, and I didn't know why. I started looking at that and thinking, 'Huh. I don't really like her. She's not a nice person.'"

Rose struggled through her three months. Without the daily drama of her mother's life, she was forced to look at her own patterns, and she didn't like what she saw. "I realized I had been a thirty-five-year-old woman calling her mommy every day," she said.

"I knew things weren't okay, but I kept being in that unhealthy environment. It made me so sad to see that even though I had moved out of my parents' house, I was still that little kid hoping for my mom and dad's approval. The price is way too high."

The feelings of sadness and anger you've been facing as you look at your abuse may intensify as you see how your abuser(s) react to your determination to be healthy and free. People cling and cling to the idea that the miracle will come and the good parents they were supposed to have will suddenly appear in the bodies of our abusers. They pretend the angry, controlling mother or father who runs their life with threats is a best friend. And it's painful when the lifelong habits that have been keeping these illusions in place slip away and my clients begin to see the situation for what it is.

Please use the strategies in chapter 5 to soothe yourself and the child if your emotions rise. Comfort the child first, and investigate the roots of your strong feelings instead of pushing them away.

Protect this sacred three months, and use this time to discover who you are when you're free of the confusing and harmful messages from the family. The work in the coming chapters is best done while you're on your hiatus from your parents/abusers. You'll be building the skills and strength you'll need to deal with the abuser(s) and non-protector(s) from a place of clarity.

To do this work, you can't abandon your truth or yourself. You must be 100 percent on your side, and respond to people based on fact, not fantasy. To protect your child, you need to see the abuser(s) for what they are, and after ninety days away, your vision will be much clearer.

When clients seem confused and cling to the belief that all will be well if they just do what the abusers want and treat them with golden-rule manners, as they'd like to be treated, I remind them about rattlesnakes. Say you fall in love with a diamondback rattler at an exotic animal fair and decide to bring it home. You feed it its favorite foods, turn up the sun lamp just the way the snake likes it, and watch as a kind of bond seems to develop between the snake and you. You start getting closer to the snake. Great. You've charmed it. Your love and care have worked a miracle, and this "fearsome thing" people have warned you about is tamed. It's your pet.

But one day you dangle lunch toward it as usual, and instead of going for the food it sinks its fangs into you. What happened? It's a rattlesnake. *Injecting its venom is what it does.* No matter how nicely you treat it, and no matter how much you imagine it would never strike you, the one who cares for it so well, the truth is if you get too close, it'll bite you. You can keep it as a pet, but you have to keep it in a glass cage, where you can see it and know it for what it is, not be lulled into thinking it's a cute puppy that can't hurt you. You have to protect yourself with distance and wary handling.

The same goes for your abuser(s) and non-protector(s). Their behavior has been, and continues to be, poisonous. Its effects have created pain and turmoil in your life, and further exposure will keep your child in peril. The child wants to reach his or her hand into the box and tempt the venom, and your responsibility is to remove the child from danger. Remember: You are not taking this break to punish your abuser(s). You are taking a time-out to heal and to protect your child. This isn't optional; it's imperative. It's a matter of life and death.

When you walk into the relationship again after your three months away, you'll have the distance to see what's really going on, and you'll be able to discern exactly what kind of boundaries you need to put in place with the abuser(s), both emotionally and physically, to keep your child safe. Your redrawn map of the relationship will reflect who they are, what your child needs, and who you have become.

9

GETTING PAST VICTIMHOOD

My clients often question at this point in the process: "Why am I still digging all this up now? What's the point? Why not just stop now that I get the picture?"

The short answer is that you had a reason for beginning this work, a reason that hasn't suddenly disappeared. It's not as though you were having a great life and suddenly said, "Gee, I think I'll do some inner-child work." The strong, healthy part of you saw a chance to ease your pain—the pain you're seeing so clearly now. It pushed you to change the script and begin to make things better. It wanted to take charge and stop being a victim. That's the impulse that will continue to drive your healing: getting past victimhood.

Chances are you don't like the "victim" label. No one does. But your child was victimized, and the effects have followed you through every phase of your life, as we saw when we chronicled its aftereffects in the early pages of this book.

It's vital to understand what it means to be a victim: The child had no choices, no options. Adults have every advantage in physical, psychological, and social power over the children they abuse. The perpetrators control the situation, and bear all responsibility for it—though, as we've seen, they work hard to make their targets believe otherwise.

At this stage, even with all the work we've done around responsibility, it may still be difficult to release the image of yourself as the one who caused all the pain you experienced, the one who deserved it. That message has been directed at you for most of your life, and you may hear a part of yourself insisting you are too defective to mend, and therefore there's no point in trying to fix the life that was ruined in childhood.

That's the voice of the victim, the helpless one who believes the abuser(s)' lies—the child who's still locked in the dark. You can recognize the victim's presence in your mind when you have thoughts like: "What good will it do?" and "It won't make any difference" and "Nothing I do will matter."

But as you continue to do the work of healing the child, and persist in countering the perpetrators' "official story" by putting responsibility for the abuse on them, where it belongs, it becomes impossible to believe your child is either blameworthy or irreparably broken. As you look into the innocent face of the child you were, and give that boy or girl the love he or she has always deserved, you can't continue to buy the lie that the child is worthless and put everyone else's needs first, either. Not as a good, loving parent of your child-self.

The child you were was, without question, a victim whose wounds you must tend. But as an adult recovering from childhood abuse, you can—and must—see yourself as much more than the victim you have been. One of the abuser(s)' most damaging legacies is the way their abuse has defined you. But when you find the courage to rewrite their script, you can grow beyond those tight confines and thrive.

As you free your adult self of victimization, a world of possibilities opens up. So let's leave behind the trap of victimhood, step-by-step.

WHAT DOES IT MEAN TO BE A VICTIM?

The original meaning of victim was "a person or animal killed as a sacrifice," and that definition is an interesting window into what it's like to be a victim of childhood abuse. You weren't killed, of course, but it's no stretch to say you were sacrificed—your original self, with all its possibilities, was overpowered by people who considered themselves and their needs to be much more important and worthy than yours. Your abuser(s) were like the reckless, destructive gods of old myths who took what they wanted because they could. They had the power to take your innocence, your joy, your sense of confidence and ease, leaving you with shame and guilt and insecurity— and they did. Then they justified their actions by blaming you.

When you are a child, you don't have the resources to challenge the "gods" in your life who are abusing you. They're bigger, stronger, more believable, more respected than you are. They're supposed to be right. So you search for ways to make the abuse make sense. "Why did it happen?" the child asks. "Because the big people were worthy of doing whatever they wanted, and I am worthless. Because I'm bad. Because I'm nothing, I'm powerless."

Pay attention to these words as they flit through your head or appear in your writing: "I'm bad. I'm nothing. I'm worthless. I have no power." This is the voice of the victim.

Mike, the graphic artist who'd faced sexual abuse and neglect, began listening for victim words, victim labels, and he was stunned to find so many. "I thought that I was my biggest advocate, with getting sober and overcoming my childhood by getting a good job and all these things," he told me. "It wasn't clear to me how much damage I was doing to myself with these old thoughts, and how much I had been holding myself back—and how much power I had to change my life."

It may seem counterintuitive, but you begin to tap that power by recognizing that you were a victim, and looking for ways you continue to be.

Some people, maybe most, don't want to linger around the word "victim." They'd rather skip it in favor of calling themselves survivors. But slapping a happy-face sticker that says "survivor" over the pain the child experienced doesn't fix anything. It doesn't let you address the experiences and beliefs of the victimized child you were. Yes, you are a survivor, and there's much to be said for that. You made it through hell, and that took incredible resilience. Yet surviving with all the aftereffects of abuse isn't recovery. You deserve the true liberation that's earned by coming to terms with the pain of having been a victim, and doing the hard job of working through it, until you reach the freedom on the other side. That requires naming and claiming the identity of victim for your child. "Victim" is the correct label for what the child became because of the abuse, and using it for the child validates his or her experience. "Yes," it says, "what happened was bad. It hurt you. It left you with injuries we need to heal."

IT'S TIME TO PUT YOURSELF FIRST

To help the child, though, you—the adult who's responsible for your recovery and the child's—can't stay caught in the passivity and powerlessness of victimhood. Can you hear the echoes of the victim's voice—"I'm bad," "I'm a fuck-up," "I haven't got what it takes"—in your life today? Recognizing that voice, and the pain it continues to bring the child inside, is a first step in getting past victimization. Then you must challenge that voice and change the way you respond to it.

Victimization taught you to say, "I don't count," and one sure sign you're operating from that belief is valuing other people more highly than you value yourself, always putting their needs first, and placing yourself last in line. Generosity is a virtue, and it's important to help other people and be there for them. But it's easy to lose yourself in what looks like altruism and good deeds, and to keep erasing yourself from the list of people who need your resources and kindness.

You don't do anyone any favors by working yourself into the ground to serve other people's agendas. You wind up so depleted you can't help anyone. You're rebuilding your foundation in this work, and I'd like you to do your best to keep your focus on yourself. I want you to make it your top priority to keep taking excellent, compassionate care of yourself and your child, and to keep your energy and attention directed toward your own deepest desire: the desire to heal. If you want to help others in a meaningful way, you first need to take control of the agenda and do what's required to make *yourself* strong, healthy, and positive.

I know you may struggle to put yourself first. And I know you may have tried and failed many times to do what you've said you'd do for yourself. But your relationship with your child is changing you. The more time you spend imagining the child, listening to the child, even falling in love with the child, the more you'll feel compelled to put his or her needs above all else. You may be doubtful and full of self-criticism when your actions don't match your intent, upset when you "get busy" and forget the child. But you've come a long way already, and I know you can keep going despite your doubts.

Put your best effort, day by day by day, behind your commitment to recover. Doing that is a statement to yourself, your child, and the world: "I want to be whole and healed. I want that more than anything, and I am *worthy* of having it."

That is the voice of the adult who has chosen not to be a victim any longer, an adult who has taken 100 percent responsibility for his or her own healing.

DON'T LET DOUBT STOP YOU

If you have doubts about your ability to stay on this path, write them down. Then ask the healthy adult part of yourself—or a higher power, if you believe in one—to take charge as you do this work. Every time you fight doubt, ask for help, or challenge the victim voices that tell you you can't or don't deserve to heal, you take a giant step toward leaving victimization behind.

I'd like to share a powerful piece of writing Mike did at about this point in the work. As you read, you may recognize some of your own hopes and fears:

> I feel like such a fraud and it angers me. I want my pain to be someone else's fault. So that my anger is justified. And so I don't have so much guilt. But the truth remains, they're my demons causing the pain and anger.
>
> I'm afraid I am going to ruin this life I have been blessed with. I'm tired of being at this same place over and over and never really learning or changing. All talk no action.
>
> I'm tired of feeding myself lies not even I believe anymore. I'm selfish and disloyal. I fear being hurt and abandoned and in turn I hurt those close to me and push them away before they can leave.
>
> If there was ever a time in my life to grow past this plateau, that time is now. I have an amazing partner who wants so desperately to make me happy. And who I truly love with all my heart.
>
> I need to love myself enough to know I actually deserve this life. But instead I do things that make me feel bad and dirty to prove that in fact I don't deserve anything.
>
> I want to change but I'm afraid that I won't be able to.

And if I can, for how long? There's always a breaking point, the point of fuck it!

Please God help me. Help me get out of my own way and grow into the man you'd have me be. Prove me wrong. Prove that I can do this, and I can grow and change with your help.

If you're asking yourself, "What will be different this time? How will I get past the point where I've always turned back, 'the point of fuck it'?" I can tell you what I told Mike:

- Your love for your child is growing, and it is changing both your heart and your brain.
- You are learning to face your feelings, honestly and courageously, instead of burying them.
- You are absolutely clear about your desire to heal.
- You are choosing, right now, to commit to yourself, and you can renew that commitment any time you feel shaky or discouraged. You are no longer a victim.

I can't overstate the power of the commitment you are making to your healing, and I'd like you to put it front and center now.

ASSIGNMENT 1: Post Your Commitment Message

Write these words on a piece of paper: "Today, I keep my commitments to myself."

Tape this message to your bathroom mirror, fridge, the dashboard of your car, or wherever you will see it regularly. It will remind you that you are going to walk your talk and show up for yourself.

Please do this now, and don't continue until you have

put the message in several places where you can see it often. Read it aloud to yourself.

Use it to check in with yourself whenever you notice it. What commitments have you made to yourself and your child? How will you honor them today?

CLAIMING YOUR TRUE IDENTITY

Moving beyond a victim identity is a process of learning to question the "truths" of the past and to enter the present as an empowered, self-defining adult. This will take persistence, because you've identified yourself, consciously or unconsciously, as a victim for so long—the whole of your life since the abuse.

Now I'd like you to reclaim the timeline of your life by looking at the abuse you faced as a series of events that began and ended in the past. Those events changed the course of your life for a time and took you in a direction you were not meant to go. They kept you from knowing yourself and being all you could be.

You were a victim of those events, and you're living with the painful effects of those crimes—yet there's much more to you than the label "victim" can describe. And as you stand in this moment, your identity is much larger, richer, and more powerful than the one imprinted on you as the abuse events were happening, the ones with the insults, slaps, and slurs attached.

I know it may still seem almost impossible to escape the identity the abuser(s) imposed on you, even when it is clearly a wild distortion of who you are. That distorted picture is intimately familiar, and it has been reinforced so constantly by the abuser(s) that it has become the mirror in which you see yourself and the script that guides your life. Because of that, you may have felt frozen inside a destiny—victimhood—you could not escape. "No escape." "No choice." That's the victim mentality that has robbed you of your power and kept you perpetually stuck in the story of the past.

So let's shift the script about who you are and who you can be. Who are you when you're a victim? And more important, who are you when you're not? When you gain clarity about both those iden-tities, you can finally choose the one that is rightfully yours—the one that's untainted by the abuser(s)' lies and distortions. You'll have the power to define yourself.

THE VOICE THAT DISPARAGES AND SAYS "GIVE UP" IS THE VOICE OF THE ABUSER. TURN IT OFF.

Your abuser(s) have handed you a script that makes you both the victim and the abuser. They've called you degrading names and lied about your worth, and you've kept those insults alive by believing they are true, and repeating them to yourself. *Those beliefs continue the abuse.*

How much of the way you think of yourself and the world is built on the lies and insults you internalized from your abuser(s)? Take a minute to recall the names you've been called, the labels meant to sum you up and dismiss your value and importance. The shorthand ways of saying: "You deserved the pain you got." The abuser(s) used words such as "loser," "whore," "slut," "fag." Words such as "stupid," "ugly," "lazy," "worthless," "piece of shit."

I'm sure you can think of plenty more words chosen to make you feel small. "Who do you think you are? You'll never amount to anything. I wish I never had you. You ruined my life."

These proclamations, coming from the all-powerful abusers, seem true to the children, who accept them and think this is how others see them, and how they really are. More damningly, children think the way others see them is *all they'll ever be.* And that crushes them, heart and soul. No one who believes such things about them-selves feels worthy of anything good in the world. Others don't think they deserve love and happiness—how can they feel good about their lives?

But these words, these labels, don't belong to you, and you have the power now to stop them from defining you and to protect the child inside you from their abusive messages. It's your responsibility to pay attention to the voices in your mind and to challenge the ones that shame and defame you, the ones that tell you to give up because you can't change. They're like holograms that seem alive but disappear when you flick off their power source. Every time you turn away from the lies and replace them with the truth of who you are, they grow fainter. And the child inside stands taller.

The following assignments will help you see and replace the lies of victimhood. Please set aside some uninterrupted time to do this important writing. It will help give you new words for describing and thinking about who you are and who you want to be.

ASSIGNMENT 2: How Have You Contributed to the Abuse?

It is difficult, and painful, to admit you have played a role in allowing the abuse to continue by accepting the beliefs of your abuser(s). But part of leaving victimhood behind involves identifying the ways in which you've participated in the abuse of the child inside you, and choosing to stop.

Take a moment now to write a short list of the false beliefs about yourself you've accepted until now—the lies and insults that came from your abuser(s)—and how they've affected your life.

Mike's list had items such as:

- I spent years telling myself that I'm dirty. And then spent years putting myself in situations that made me feel dirty.

- I told myself that I was dumb and ugly.
- I told myself people were lying when they said they loved me.
- I've beaten myself up when I've failed at something.

When you reach the end of your list, write: "I choose not to accept these beliefs, which do not serve me. I commit to challenging these old ways of being."

Treat yourself gently and with understanding as you unplug from the abuser(s)' harmful programming. Taking responsibility for your recovery means expanding your awareness and changing what needs to be changed, not blaming yourself for what you didn't know.

ASSIGNMENT 3: Actively Challenge the Abusers' Labels

Now I'd like you to take direct aim at the abuser(s)' lies by countering them with the truth about the child inside.

Draw a vertical line down the middle of a piece of paper, creating two columns. Label the left column "What they called me," and in it, list all the terrible thoughts you think about yourself and that you heard spoken about you when you were a child. Write down all the adjectives, insults, and negative attributes you've been saddled with all these years.

Label the right column with the words "What I really am," and for each negative thought, write a statement about yourself that describes the real you, the person you believe your best self to be. For every negative adjective, quality, or attribute you listed, offer yourself and your child a positive adjective, quality, or attribute that reflects your truth.

If you have trouble coming up with positives, think of

how you would reassure and comfort your child if a bully called him or her names. It's okay if you don't yet fully believe the positive statements you're writing in the "What I really am" column. What would you like the truth to be? That's the new freedom we're aiming for, and those are the seeds we're planting in you, and in the child, with this work.

Your list might look something like this:

WHAT THEY CALLED ME	WHAT I REALLY AM
Stupid	I am a smart, creative person.
Ugly	I am beautiful with all my imperfections. I'm perfect just the way I am.
Whore	I am a person whose sexuality is sacred and worthy of respect.
Piece of shit	I am a person of great value.
Loser	I am a success.

Put this paper in a place where you will see it, or fold it up and put it in your wallet. When you hear the old labels and lies coming up, pay attention. Stop them. Pull out your list and answer them with the truth of who you really are.

ASSIGNMENT 4: Discuss the List With Your Child

After you make your list, discuss your feelings with your child. With your dominant hand, write to your child and ask if she or he wants to talk about some of these words and thoughts. You, the good parent, must let this child know that none of the labels are true, and that none of the insults have anything to do with what he or she did. Tell your child, "You do not deserve these insults. You are not any of these bad things. You deserve a good parent and a good life." Remind the child that you are there, working and learning to be that good parent. Speak right to the heart of your child.

Then answer with your nondominant hand, and let your child speak.

ASSIGNMENT 5: "If You Really Knew Me . . ."

I know I'm asking you to do a lot, but I want you to have plenty of ammunition for fighting the lies that have been the soundscape of your life. So I'd like you to do one more bit of private writing, addressed to yourself, the abuser(s), and the people in your world. Start with the words "If you really knew me," and describe your true self, free of the abuser(s)' labels. You know the fullness of who you are, though it's been hidden and you are only now beginning to express it. Be as open as you can. Embrace yourself, the light and the dark. As you'll see in the following examples, both Rose and Mike found ways to look at themselves kindly, unblinkingly, and honestly. That's what I hope you will do.

Here's what Rose wrote:

If you really knew me you would know that I am a worrywart and think bad things will happen. I tend to look at the negative, worst-case scenario before I even consider the positive side. I doubt myself a lot and am extremely afraid of failure. Sometimes I don't pursue a goal because I already have played out the outcome in my head.

If you really knew me you would know that I am very strong. I keep going even if at times it seems like I am giving up. I get up from the slump and keep going. Once I put my focus into accomplishing a goal I am unwavering. I have a lot of knowledge that I can contribute to my community. I may be lazy at times and be unmotivated. That time passes and I am right back on track.

Mike's list looked like this:

If you really knew me you'd know I'm terrified of failure.

You'd know I'm financially insecure.

You'd know I'm judgmental and slightly racist.

If you really knew me you'd know I so desperately want to be rescued.

You'd know that I'm entitled and selfish.

You'd know that I think about me much more than I do about you.

If you really knew me you'd know that my sexuality scares me.

You'd know that staying faithful is a struggle.

You'd know I live 80% of my life in my head.

You'd know that I seek your approval.

If you really knew me you'd know I'm shy and nervous with a mask of confidence.

If you really knew me, you'd know that I take everything personally.

That I have a hard time with confrontation.

That I worry people will abandon me.

If you really knew me you'd know it's hard for me to trust.

If you really knew me, you'd know that I'm working every day to be the best me that I can be.

You'd know that when I love I love with all my heart.

When I give I give all of me.

When I say I'll do something I do it.

When I want something I work for it.

When I'm scared I turn to God.

When I'm lonely I think of how full my life is. And when I doubt that I deserve good I tell doubt to fuck off. I'm glad I know me.

When you write honestly about yourself, it can be a little startling to realize the way you are is okay. You don't have to hide either your weaknesses or your strengths from yourself. You're not the failed, flawed person of your abuser(s)' lies, and you're not some artificial piece of fake, flawless perfection. You're human. What a relief.

YOU ARE RESPONSIBLE FOR GETTING UP WHEN YOU FALL

As you work to keep your commitments to yourself by nurturing yourself and your child, and challenging the abuser(s)' lies whenever they come up, you're going to make a few mistakes from time to time, take a few steps backward. You may forget a promise to your child and have to apologize and make good. You may fall back into an old pattern and have to recommit to making new choices. That's okay. As human beings, we are not perfect. The goal is progress, not perfection.

Perfection, of course, is impossible. But the bigger problem with the word is this: It's only useful for assessing where you've been, not as a guide to the path in front of you. The words—the values—that will help light your way as you leave victimhood behind are "hope," "courage," "commitment," "work," and "truth."

Your commitment to this work and to yourself will change your life forever. The important thing is to be on your child's side an hour at a time, a day at a time. Follow through, step-by-step. Get back up when you fall. I know you won't ever give up, because all you need is a small spark of hope bright enough to illuminate the next healthful choice, and the next. You've got that. You picked up this book. You're taking the risk of changing.

If you make a mistake? So be it! That's expected. Just dust yourself off and keep going. The secret of success in life is getting up every time you fall. The same resilience that's brought you this far will see you through to the finish line.

GIVING UP VICTIMHOOD DOESN'T COME WITHOUT LOSSES

In shedding the identity and mentality of a victim, you can finally unload the debilitating burden of the labels and lies that have warped your sense of who you are and what's possible for you. But you'll also have to give up some parts of your life that may have given you refuge and comfort.

Letting go of the victim role means:

- YOU CAN'T BLAME EVERYTHING THAT GOES WRONG ON YOUR PAST. Defining yourself as a victim has given you a go-to excuse for everything that's gone wrong since the abuse. Bad job? "The abuse turned me loose on the world unprepared—and there's nothing I can do about it." Bad relationships? "The abuse screwed me up—and nothing's going to change that."

As we've seen, you can trace much that's not working in your life to the aftereffects of the abuse you suffered. But de-victimizing yourself means giving up the helpless stance and deciding you can do plenty to heal.

Lisa, who was sexually abused by her father and brother, put it this way: "When you've truly been victimized, it's hard not to live as a victim. I didn't always see my part in things. I thought, 'The world owes me.' But I'm the one who owes me. I'm the one who can change."

You're the one who must take responsibility for what's happening in your life now, and look to yourself to repair what's broken. You'll also need to keep making the distinction: The abuse wasn't your fault. But you are 100 percent responsible for recovering from it. There's astonishing power in that.

- YOU'LL HAVE TO STOP WAITING FOR SOMEONE TO RESCUE YOU. Until now, you bought into the view of yourself that you were powerless, and looked outside yourself for someone who could save you and tell you what to do. A hero who would swoop in, slay your demons, and make everything all better. Now, though, you'll have to learn to become an individual who can stand on your own two feet and trust yourself. It's a global shift, to stop waiting. Finally, you can move ahead and live your own life.

It will take sustained effort to stop believing the only choice open to you is to suffer as a silent victim, and to see the world of options open to you. I think about stories I've heard about elephants that have been chained to a pole and only able to walk in a circle for months on end. That's their path in life, that single circle. And when someone runs in to remove the chain and free them from that painful, tiny world, they keep walking in the circle at first, unable to imagine stepping outside.

You may feel like that, knowing you're not a victim but not quite able to see how to step out of the circle of victimization. So I want you to imagine it. Imagine the freedom and your new way of being. You *will* do the work of freeing yourself. You're not a victim anymore.

ASSIGNMENT 5: Imagine Your Life Beyond Victimhood.

Write a letter to yourself and answer the questions: "What will I lose if I stop being a victim? What will my life look like if I take responsibility for my life?"

Here's what one of my clients wrote. Let it inspire you to envision your post-victim life and self:

Dear self,

I will miss those moments when I say to myself, "Oh what's the use? What a loser! You will never amount to anything."

I will lose the safe place of underachieving. I will lose the belief that fears rule my life. I will lose the "me" that fantasizes about being able to live, succeed, prosper, create, and love, without feeling anything, risking anything, or working hard, while abandoning myself, running away, and making myself a victim.

I will lose the "me" that makes the world responsible for the ease and magnitude of my success, comfort, emotional well-being, and financial stability.

I am my own keeper and partner now, and I'm fully responsible for the containment, love, and care of myself and all my pain, fear, discomfort, and feelings of abandonment. I am responsible for taking steps to work, create, earn, communicate, and foster a safe atmosphere in which I can risk and strive. The old idea that someone else will carry me and maintain love, consistency, safety, and opportunity is an old idea. I must take full responsibility.

To achieve career success, I must take all necessary steps along the way. I will tolerate criticism and rejection that occurs in any field of work and in day-to-day life. Waiting for luck or validation or a break from the world is a setup for me to be a victim: disappointed, resentful, and alone. I can and should ask for help, but I can never forget that the primary responsibility falls on myself.

Miracles never come in the expected form, and I will try not to anticipate them. I will take actions as if miracles never happen, and I will be astounded by their occurrence at all times, all around me.

I am not afraid to take all the necessary little steps. I don't need to take spectacular steps to go to spectacular places. My own estimable acts create the esteem I so deserve and desire.

I can do this, and I will.

Love,

Me

Remember to pace yourself as you go. Lisa's attitude was grounded and helpful: "Once I accepted that this healing would take a while," she told me, "I allowed myself to dive in and dig deep, and then rest if I needed to. I think of it like hiking—you push yourself and then take a little while to breathe. It's a marathon, not a sprint."

You can do this. You're not a victim. Keep going.

10

WORKING WITH YOUR ALLIES
The Child and the One
Who Knows

You may feel vulnerable and perhaps a little at sea as you shake your-self free of the victim role and stop looking for something outside yourself that can carry you away from the pain of the past. Yes, you want to become the empowered, de-victimized version of yourself. But the first steps can seem shaky as you look in the mirror and say, "Well, I'm it. I'm the one who gets to make this recovery happen."

Fortunately, you don't have to do it alone, struggling in the old way. You have a pair of allies who can be your sounding boards, your advisers, and your guides toward what you most need to know and do next. They're on your team as you leave victimhood behind.

The first of these allies, your child, has likely become more vivid and real to you since you began using this book. The child can be your master teacher in the emotional realm, showing you again and again what's true for you and how you really feel. Children, as you've no doubt noticed, have a simple directness adults don't. They speak from the heart, and they're not worried about protecting anyone. If they see something they don't like, they say, simply, "This is bad. This is wrong. This hurts." They love what they love without fear, and they're not afraid to announce, "This is what I want." There are no long explanations, just a direct connection to the emotional truth.

As your child feels safer, and comes to trust that you will listen, he or she will give you the benefit of succinct—and often blunt— assessments of what's happening at the feeling level as you face the kinds of challenges that may have overpowered you in the past.

Life doesn't stop just because you've decided to spend this time focusing on what happened to you when you were young. It keeps throwing you the same curveballs and surprises as always. But this time, you have the child's welfare to consider, and his or her emotional reading of the situation to help you as you field what comes your way. Each time you stop to ask, "Is this good for the child?" and seek the child's perspective on what's going on, you have a chance not only to understand the impact of your present-day actions but also to see how they register with the child and are colored by the child's perceptions. You can make new choices and act in ways that will not be blindly driven by hidden emotions.

"I'm getting so conscious of that little boy and his feelings about things," Steven, the stockbroker, told me with a surprised look on his face. "I'm starting to listen to that inner voice of 'Something doesn't feel right,' which used to go right by me before. I have that focus in my brain: My little boy's here and I'm keeping him safe. A couple of things happened last week. I was at a bar and I decided not to go home with somebody because my kid felt scared. I went to the bathroom, came out, and said I was going to go home and call it a night. And something else came up later on. I was online getting ready to buy something, and I became conscious that my little boy was feeling anxious. I got it that he was upset because spending like that just means more debt and more pressure. So I didn't push the button. It was big for me. Both those things."

Pausing to notice the child, and to listen to his or her concerns, interrupts the automatic responses and feelings the abuse wired into your brain. It builds reflective moments into your everyday life that give you a chance to bring your thinking adult self into the picture. That can change you in significant ways.

The biggest changes may come from the smallest interactions. You and the child are becoming a family, a warm home base for each other. As you show up day after day to respond to the child's concerns and provide love and comfort when difficult feelings arise, you earn the child's trust in ways you can see vividly in your right-hand/left-hand writing. And in comforting the child, you will find yourself being comforted in a new way. Pulling the child into your arms and your heart changes you. Something as small as saying "I love you" to the child morning and night, and seeing the child's "I love you" in return, slips the voices of the loving parent and the well-loved child into your ear—again and again.

I can't overstate the healing power of a hundred or a thousand "I love yous." Entry by entry, you are demonstrating to each other what consistency, affection, honesty, and trust can look like be-tween a parent and child, and you're doing it without having to wait for outside intervention or a magic wand—or for the people in your past to change.

THE WISE ONE INSIDE

Your second ally is a part of yourself I'd like to introduce to you now. I call this source of wisdom the One Who Knows, though some of my clients refer to "my wise man" or "the wise woman inside."

As you talk to the child and reassure him or her you'll keep work-ing to be a good parent, you may find yourself longing for a good parent of your own, someone to help you cut through your confusion and find your way. That is the function, and the gift, of the One Who Knows.

You make contact with the One Who Knows in the way you do with the child, by writing a question with your dominant hand and capturing the answer with your nondominant hand. I think of the One Who Knows as the ancient part of ourselves with cell memory that's been carried through the ages, from our ancestors to us. It's the collective wisdom of our lineage, available to us whenever we ask then listen for a response. The One Who knows is there for you, with no ulterior motives and no agenda but your highest good, to help you see what you most need, what you deserve, and what's possible for you, so you can bring it into your life.

You can trust that the direct, grounding advice that comes from the One Who Knows is concerned purely with your well-being.

"I have to confess, this sounds like witchcraft," said Amanda, who skeptically agreed to see what happened when she wrote to the wise woman inside her. But as her wise woman's words appeared on the page, she steadily gained confidence that she had the power within herself to heal from the emotional abuse of her controlling parents.

"When you asked me to picture her, I imagined an old woman coming to me with wisdom and gentleness," Amanda told me. "Her words aren't necessarily that different from what I might journal to myself, but she inspires me and elevates me to another level, and I don't feel alone. I have someone to look up to. My parents disappointed me because they abandoned me emotionally—I don't need to have that explained to me. I needed to have a healthy relationship to take the place of the broken one—and this is so powerful. I've always looked outside myself for that relationship, but this time I don't have to look outward. My wise woman is the archetypal mother—and she's me. It's hard to explain, but when I talk to her, I'm talking to something larger than my own mind."

The One Who Knows can calm the rushed and impatient part of you that jumps to follow an impulse or can't stop worrying about what's coming. It has the voice of your best adult self, with a wisdom that stands outside the rush of time. As Bill put it, "It's the part of you that is absolutely not confused. It's intuition. My experience is that it's less emotional than the child but just as real. The One Who Knows is the person who sees you and the situation for what they are. It speaks the truth of what it sees, unclouded by emotion."

The One Who Knows is there to support you as you support the child inside, the wise adviser who can offer you the guidance you need to stay centered and to be the best parent and person you can be.

The most common homework I give my clients is to ask the child and the One Who Knows for their perspective on a feeling or situation that's bothering them. The habit of reflecting on your experience by looking to your inner allies first, and acting on what you learn from them, only gets stronger as you use it.

CONSULTING YOUR ALLIES: ROSE'S EXPERIENCE

In my groups, members read their writing to one another and learn from one another how the child comes to life for them, and how the One Who Knows always seems to provide the words they need to hear. I'd like to give you a taste of that experience by showing you how Rose worked with the child and the One Who Knows over time, as she navigated a challenging situation in her life.

With the encouragement of the realtors she worked for, Rose took a prep class at night and finally reached the point where she was ready to take the real estate exam. She prided herself on being hard-working and self-reliant—work had always been a place to escape her pain and build a feeling of confidence in herself—and she threw herself into preparing for the test. It was tricky territory. It's easy to use outside accomplishments as ways of establishing your self-worth, and to build yourself a shaky new scaffolding of conditional love that says, "I'm okay as long as I get this job/pass this test/earn someone's praise." But healing from abuse means learning to love and have faith in yourself as you change, grow, and let new experiences shape you— to value your best efforts regardless of outcomes and conditions.

That was Rose's real test as she prepared for the exam, and her child and the One Who Knows gave her invaluable feedback and support along the way. The following journal excerpts show a "time-lapse" version of the writing Rose did in the period before and right after the test. I'm giving you a more extended look at this writing so you'll see how, by standing with the child at one shoulder and the One Who Knows at the other, you can connect with the truths that will allow you to persist, learn, and change.

"WISH WE COULD HAVE SOME FUN"

The first letter is an exchange with Little Rose, Rose's child, as Rose throws herself into studying.

> Rose: Dear Little Rose, How are you doing?
> Little Rose: I am OK.
> Rose: Is there anything you would like to talk about? How are you feeling?
> LR: I am OK. Just a little tired. We have been studying a lot. Wish we could have some fun. It seems all you do is work work and work. And now if you are not working you are studying.
> Rose: I hear you, sweetie. I know that there is little time for us to have fun together. I am studying so I can provide a better life for us. Soon we will be able to spend more time having fun. Is there anything in particular you would like us to do?
> LR: Yes, the trampoline. You said you were going to take me. I want to jump.

Rose: Sorry sweetie you are right. I have not kept my promise. I will look at our schedule and check when we can go. Is there anything else you want us to do?

LR: Yes, I want to do scrapbooking. I like decorating the pages with pictures. I think I am good at it. I want to use all the pretty stickers. I love stickers.

Rose: I think that is a great idea. I agree with you that you are good at it. I will work in some nights for us to scrapbook. As soon as I am done with the real estate exam I will sign us up for a scrapbooking class. I am excited. How much fun! How are you feeling about our working in a new office?

LR: I feel OK about it. You were pretty stressed out. But you seem relieved. You seem nicer not as grouchy.

Rose: OK sweetie. I know that I have been stressed out. I am working on ways to reduce my stress level. This week I will check in with you and see how you are doing. I love you and will take care of you.

When Rose was first getting to know Little Rose, and learning to be kind to the child inside her, she asked me what her little girl might consider to be a treat. She'd had very few treats or kindnesses when she was growing up, and at that point had given few to her adult self. I suggested that she look at what her nieces enjoyed doing, and when Rose went to a stationery shop, Little Rose discovered the world of stickers. "My little girl is all about stickers and decorated tape and pretty paper," Rose reported back. Now, Little Rose requests them—and notices when opportunities for that kind of fun, and others, such as trampoline jumping, disappear for long stretches. The child insists on balance—there's more to life, she knows, than "work work and work"—and she notices moods Rose might ignore:

"You seem nicer not as grouchy." She makes it harder for Rose to neglect her desire to live fully, even while focused on the intensity of the test. The child wants to eat. Sleep. Play. Be. Not just work.

"I DON'T LIKE TESTS"

Rose was understandably concerned about her exam, and Little Rose couldn't help but notice. The more you come in contact with the reality of your child, the more natural it becomes to speak to the child with great kindness. In acknowledging the child's concerns, and reassuring her, Rose does the same for herself. It only takes a few words.

> Rose: Dear Little Rose, How are you sweetie?
> LR: I am doing well a little nervous about the test. I don't like tests.
> Rose: Sweetie, don't worry we will try our best. I know that tests are scary and it is understandable that you would be nervous. I will be taking the test and you have nothing to worry about. Is there anything else you would like to discuss?
> LR: Not really.
> Rose: OK sweetie. I love you and I will talk to you later.
> LR: Love you too!

"I Was Feeling Anxious"

When Rose began to have trouble sleeping as the test neared, she went to the child for insights into the feelings below the insomnia. Notice how much more direct and useful this practice is than fretting to a coworker or looking outside the self for clarity. Also notice the caring tone she uses with the child. There's no scolding ("Why couldn't you be good and sleep?"), no need for false cheerfulness. This loving way of talking to the child does not fan anxieties and hot emotions or keep them circling; it soothes them at the source.

Rose: Good morning Little Rose, How are you this morning?

LR: Good morning. I am tired. I was up too late last night.

Rose: Yes sweetie. We could not go to sleep. What was that about? What were you feeling?

LR: I was feeling anxious. I feel like I missed out on a lot of opportunities academically.

Rose: I understand. We have the rest of our life to pursue our dreams and go for it. We will take one day at a time. We get to be patient. What would you like to be when you grow up?

LR: I am not sure there are so many choices. I am afraid of not making the right choice.

Rose: It is okay not to know. We get to explore all our options and we will see which option is the best for us both. How are you feeling this morning? Anything worrying you?

LR: Yes. I feel anxious and afraid that I am not doing enough in my life.

Rose: Sweetie, you don't need to worry I will take care of us. You get to play and have fun. Enjoy life, that is what you get to do. I love you very much and I plan to create a peaceful and joyful life for us.

LR: I love you too.

TURNING TO THE ONE WHO KNOWS FOR INSIGHTS AND REASSURANCE

Comforting the child brought only so much comfort to Rose, so she wrote immediately to the One Who Knows. That's what I advise, and what I'd like you to do as you work with these allies:

Take care of the child first. Comfort him or her; soothe the worries; provide attention, love, and care. Then tap the wisdom of the One Who Knows, who can give you more perspective and understanding.

Rose: To the One Who Knows: Why am I worried about my future?

The One Who Knows: You are afraid that your past will prevent you from accomplishing your future goals. You need to relax and breathe. You will be able to accomplish your goals. You just need to stay focused and practice discipline. You will succeed. Have faith.

Going to the One Who Knows bypasses the old abuser(s)' voices, which might've said things such as: "You'll never make it." "You're not good enough." And there's no trace of the victim's voice either, the "What's the use?" and "I'm doomed" that once were always at the ready. The One Who Knows, succinct and incisive, is wired to wisdom, and the truth about you.

"WE ARE IN THIS TOGETHER"

Working with the child is a long-term exercise in honesty, listening to what the child has to say, and doing your best to provide protection and love. You'll always see your hopes, fears, and behavior reflected in your child's eyes. The next two letters show how fears and patterns repeat and require ongoing attention. You can't write a couple of notes to the child, or spend a day doing right-hand/left-hand writing, and declare, "I understand the child—the healing's done." It's the day-to-day relationship that does the work and allows you to build the parent-child connection that will bring true healing.

Are you keeping promises to yourself and your child? Worrying instead of resting? The child will definitely let you know what he or she observes. At the same time, you'll probably notice how watchful and worried the child can become, and how quick to assume adult stresses and burdens. This is one of the lingering aftereffects of the abuse that robbed you of the carefree days of childhood. But now you have the power to free the child inside to be a child, and find out what can happen when that spontaneous creative energy comes alive within you.

Rose: Dear Little Rose, How are you today?

LR: I am OK. I feel anger. I am mad that I am not being productive. I seem to be daydreaming a lot.

Rose: Sweetie, you can daydream if you'd like, there is nothing wrong with daydreaming. You just need to think about yourself at the moment. I will take care of you. I am responsible for our well-being. I will make sure I am productive to take good care of us. What else is bothering you?

LR: I am afraid that we won't have enough money to pay the bills. I am afraid.

Rose: Sweetie, don't be afraid. We get to have faith that everything will be okay. We will make it through. We have gone through many more difficult things. This will pass. The anxiety and insecurity. What other feelings are you having?

LR: I feel anxious. I want to run. I feel like I am getting nowhere.

Rose: Sweetie we've got to be patient. Rome was not built in one day. It takes time. We've got to give ourselves time to heal and reflect. We're taking it easy.

We will keep moving forward. I love you sweetie
and we are in this together. Anything else you want
to discuss?

LR: No I love you too.

Rose: Okay, love you. Goodbye. (smiley face)

Part of Rose's development as a good parent has involved learning to pay attention to little Rose and follow up, rather than ignoring what she says. Like her, you can learn to ask your child: "What else is bothering you?" and "What other feelings are you having?" and "Anything else you want to discuss?" You can dig, just as a good parent would, for what may be waiting to be expressed. Just be prepared for the honesty that will flow your way. The child, once assured of your attention, will not hold back.

Rose: Dear Little Rose, Good morning love of my life.
How are you today?

LR: I'm OK.

Rose: I notice that you were uncomfortable yesterday
when we went to hear music at the concert.

LR: Yes, there were too many people. I wanted to come
home. I was tired.

Rose: Ok sweetie, I understand. It seems like you have
been tired a lot lately. Can you share with me why
you think you are so tired?

LR: Yes, you are constantly worrying about money. It's
tiring. Your mind thinks, thinks, thinks. We are not
resting and quieting our mind.

Rose: Little Rose, you don't need to worry or think about
money. I will take care of us. I promise you that.

LR: Promises, promises, promises. You are not good at
keeping promises.

> Rose: I admit I am not good at keeping promises. What
> I can tell you with confidence is that I am working
> on it. Eventually I know that I will be able to keep
> my promises no matter what. In the meantime,
> thank you for being patient and sharing with me
> your feelings. I really do appreciate it. Is there any-
> thing else you want to talk about?
> LR: Yes, I want to go to the trampoline this weekend.
> Rose: OK, I will make sure we do that. Love you sweetie.
> LR: Love you too! (frog sticker)

WORKING THROUGH DISAPPOINTMENT

After months of studying, Rose took the real estate exam, and like half the people who do, she failed on her first attempt. But she kept checking in with her child, and with the One Who Knows to gain perspective on her feelings.

The victim you once were knows well how to blame any discomfort on the past and could easily fall into the pattern of facing any disappointments by echoing the abuser(s)' words: "I'm not good enough." "I don't have what it takes." "I've always been a failure." Your child and the One Who Knows, though, have a different agenda. They're most concerned with helping you identify what you need to recover—rest, fun, encouragement, belief in yourself— and prodding you to correct your course to find it. Watch them at work in the following writing.

> Rose: Dear Little Rose, How are you feeling?
> LR: I am scared. I feel out of control. I feel like things
> are not well.
> Rose: Why are you scared?
> LR: I am scared because you are angry and frustrated.

Rose: OK sweetie I am sorry for how I have been acting and for scaring you. It was not my intention to scare. I am scared myself. My feelings seemed to get the best of me. I appreciate you being honest with me and letting me know how you feel. I will work on reducing my stress and frustration. I love you.

RB: I love you too.

• • •

Rose: Dear Little Rose, Hi sweetie. How are you today?

LR: I am OK. I am feeling better.

Rose: Is there anything you would like to talk about?

LR: Yes, you promised we would do something fun and we have not. I want to do the trampoline.

Rose: Yes, I know you do. I have not forgotten. I am trying to squeeze it into our schedule. We will go and I know I promised you that. I will keep my promise. Is there anything else bothering you?

LR: No, I am tired and want to go to bed.

Rose: OK sweetie we will go to bed then. I love you and have a good night.

LR: Love you too.

• • •

Rose: To the one who knows. Why am I feeling so depressed and tired?

The One Who Knows: You are discouraged by not passing the exam. Don't give up. Have faith that you will pass. You will become a broker. You are worthy! Just keep going. Breathe and smile. You got this. Be proud of yourself. Enjoy the process. You are a winner.

• • •

"Don't Get Discouraged"

Though she was doing the hard work of looking at her abuse and how it had affected her life, Rose decided to try once more to take the licensing test. While her little girl gave her consistent feedback that she was feeling the strain of doing too much, the One Who Knows had only one message when Rose asked, "Will I pass?" "Yes," came the reply, "you will if you work for it."

> Rose: Dear Little Rose, How are you sweetie?
> LR: I am OK. I feel tired.
> Rose: You have been tired lately. Why do you feel so tired?
> LR: I am tired because we don't get enough sleep.
> Rose: I am sorry that I am not allowing you to go to sleep early enough to get a good night sleep.

• • •

> Rose: To the One Who Knows, Why am I staying up so late and unable to go to sleep?
> The One Who Knows: You are terrified of failing. Relax, you will pass. Continue to study. Take care of yourself. Eat and sleep well. You got this. You really do.

• • •

> Rose: To The One Who Knows, Am I going to pass the exam?

The One Who Knows: Rose be patient. You will pass the exam. You will be a real estate broker. You keep going and give it your best. You are on the right path.

• • •

Rose: Dear Little Rose, How are you doing this morning?

LR: I am doing well. I am a little tired. I did have lots of fun giving out candy last night.

Rose: I am glad you enjoyed seeing the kids in costume and asking for candy. I had lots of fun too. I wanted to ask you why you think we are having anxiety. What is it all about?

LR: I am afraid that you are not working a lot. It makes me nervous and uneasy.

Rose: OK, sweetie, what can I do to make you feel at ease and not nervous?

LR: You can talk to me more and not ignore me. I have feelings too.

Rose: I am sorry if you feel like I am ignoring you. That is not my intention. I will make an effort to sit down and talk to you more. I do appreciate you being open and honest about your feelings. Is there anything else you want me to do for you?

LR: Yes, I want to go on the trampoline like you had promised.

Rose: OK, I hear you. I will research the info this weekend and schedule it for next week. I am not making any promises but I will look into it. Love you and talk to you later.

LR: Love you too.

The Victory Is in Being Kind to Yourself, and Getting Back Up

Rose's second attempt at the real estate exam failed, but it was clear to me when I heard her talk about it that she had not failed at all. She treated herself with gentleness and respect, and thought about the best way to proceed. Afterward, she told Little Rose:

> Sweetie, We tried our best. I believe that things happen for a reason and maybe we will be embarking on a better more fun journey. We don't know what life has to bring us in the future. We will be OK. You are not dumb. On the contrary you are a bright little girl. You are allowed to make mistakes and to create wonderful things. You are a talented young girl. And now you are allowed to spread your wings with no fear.

How easy it could have been, in the years before she began this work, for Rose to simply give up in the face of another disappointment. But she was becoming a master of paying attention to the old doubts, feelings, and labels when they popped up, and facing them head-on. Like everyone else who is faithful to this work, you will too.

ASSIGNMENT 1: Get to Know the One Who Knows

Today, go to the One Who Knows with a question about something you're concerned about. You might ask, "Am I doing the right thing in [situation X]?" or say something like, "I'm feeling guilty about not seeing my parents. What can I do?"

Write your question with your dominant hand, and then pause, breathing deeply, connecting with the wisest part of yourself. Let the One Who Knows reply through your nondominant hand. Remember that the One Who

Knows is there for you, to provide insights devoted solely to your betterment.

Make a point this week of consulting the One Who Knows whenever you are confused or unclear about what to do next.

ASSIGNMENT 2: Keep the Conversation Going

The work we have ahead is challenging. We'll be looking once more at the past, thinking about the abuser(s), and spending more time with the painful truths about what happened to you. Before we do, I'd like you to spend as much time as you need building your foundation with your child and the One Who Knows. Take at least a couple of weeks to work with the child through your daily check-ins and through the practice of questioning strong feelings when they come up. You don't have to spend hours doing this. Just keep your photo of your child where you can see it and give yourself the opportunity to hear the voice of your direct, funny, honest little boy or girl. Practice responding to the child with the same kind of kindness, patience, and love you saw in Rose's writing.

Address the child's concerns first. Then, when you need to, turn to the One Who Knows for clarity. Talk to both of them about what's happening in your life. Involve them in your decision making. Let them love and help you. And when they feel real to you, continue to the next chapter.

11

SAY A FINAL GOOD-BYE
to the Fantasy of a
Dramatic Rescue

As you do the everyday work of healing and taking responsibility for your recovery from abuse, a funny thing can happen. Though you know what you need to do, and you're making great progress in keeping your commitments to yourself and your child, you may bump up against an old fantasy that's particularly hard to shake.

Bill, the accountant, put it most clearly when he told me, "Yes, things are going great, even all that right-hand/left-hand stuff. This really works. And I keep wondering: 'When can I stop doing it?'" There was a part of him, he said, that was still standing back and waiting for someone to show up who could *really* fix things for good. "I feel like I keep looking for that person so I can go, 'Hi, nice to meet you. Would you like to take over?'" he said.

The fantasy of a rescue, and habit of waiting for it, are so firmly entrenched that they can subtly hold on as default ways of navigating your life unless you carefully and consistently push them away.

They're companions from your childhood, and you've long turned to them for comfort.

Children don't have the power to stop the abuse, so they wait for someone to intercede, someone who will see their pain and yell, "I will right this terrible wrong," then make everything better. "I was hoping my mom would see the pain in my face and ask me what was going on, or even ask why my grades had suddenly dropped," people often tell me. "I always hoped my dad wouldn't roll his eyes when my mother was beating me. I was sure he was going to tell her to stop."

Through the months or years of abuse, and long after, the child inside nurtures the fantasy that someday, someone will see how much he or she has suffered and come to set things right. That yearning, that expectation, clings to the child as if to say, "If there's justice, there will be a rescue." The protectors who weren't there for them when they were little will miraculously wake up, or come forward. Prince or Princess Charming will ride in on a gleaming white horse and take them away to a long-awaited happily ever after.

"Waiting was my entire life," Mike said. "I was sure God would eventually send someone to save me. I had to keep moving like a shark to find that person, and they'd fix everything. I kept thinking, 'Someone is going to come. They'll rescue me and make me okay.'"

But even when charming princes and princesses do ride in to "take care of everything," the cost of that rescue mission is enormous because it's based on an implicit assumption: They—not you—are the ones who know what's best for you and how to "fix the problem." So you sign your life over to them in return for a false sense of safety.

Of course, they'll always disappoint you because they're not you, and they *can't* know exactly what you need. You may not know what you need either, because when you never value your own judgment and abilities as much as someone else's, there *is* no you. You're the empty space at the center of a life. For the sake of a powerful rescue fantasy that puts someone else forever in control, you've essentially wiped yourself off the map.

Keep in mind that hoping to be rescued was a survival skill for the child, a way of holding on to the idea that he or she was worth saving, and that someone would recognize that. As the child feels safer, protected by you, he or she will increasingly relax into the present rather than waiting for someone else's intervention. But old ways of thinking persist. So as well as working to calm the child's need for a rescue, we also need to give your healthy adult self ways of countering the false logic embedded in the rescue fantasy.

We'll do that by examining its source, the big lie that may still persist in your mind, keeping you trapped in helplessness and a limbo of "wishing and waiting."

According to the big lie, there was a cause-and-effect relationship between your behavior and the abuse. Your "badness" was behind the way your abuser(s) treated you, and if you could only be good enough, you could magically turn your abuser(s) and the people who failed to protect you into the fantasy "good parents" you always wanted. We'll look at the dynamics that keep that belief alive, despite all you know about who's really responsible for the abuse, and I'll show you the paradoxical ways in which you may have tried to earn your rescue by directing your energy toward rescuing everyone—including your abuser(s)—except your child.

This is the truth you must hear and repeat until you feel it in your soul: Abusers do what they do because of who *they* are. You were not abused because of who you were or anything you did. Nothing you could've done, nothing you will do, can turn a person who hurt or failed to protect you into one who did.

But you have the power to step into the enormous shoes of the hero, and to deliver to your child the rescue he or she has dreamed of for so many years. You're ready.

THE FANTASY GAME

The "good parent" fantasy doesn't float in from fairy tales. It's produced and nurtured by the abuser, who manipulates the child's understanding of why the abuse is happening.

"You're making me do something I don't want to do," the abuser says to the child. "Don't make me get my belt." In prefacing the abuse with words like this, the abusers cast their harmful behavior as an unavoidable reaction provoked by some "problem" in the child, rather than admitting that they're deliberately choosing to engage in physical or emotional violence. But the child doesn't hear the rationalization. He or she takes the abuser's words literally. "I made this happen," the child thinks. "I made him rape me." "I did something to cause the beating."

The child comes to believe that if this is true—if the child can *cause* trusted caregivers to act badly—then he or she can also make them act with kindness and respect. So the child tries hard to be "good," and believes if he or she can only do that to the abuser's satisfaction, the abuse will end.

Sometimes this seems to work. A peaceful stretch may come. For a time, the abuser may be distracted by work or become sober and remorseful or pause the abuse for any number of reasons unrelated to the child. But the child reads this respite as confirmation that his or her efforts worked. Every time the child's ongoing attempts seem to pay off, the child's mistaken belief in his or her effectiveness grows.

The on-again, off-again nature of the abuse—inevitable because even the worst abuser can't continue non-stop—hooks the child on the fantasy that the good caregiver exists and will one day come back forever. So the child is always on the lookout for that loving caregiver, and trying to coax him or her out of hiding.

Children have a wonderful way of being optimistic. They

persist and persist in trying to fix their families, believing their efforts on this new day could change everything—they'll finally be good enough to end the abuse for good. They cling to the comforting lie: "I can make my abuser change if I just behave and/or do the right thing."

The illusion persists into adulthood. Most of my clients can't seem to let go of the wishful thinking. They can't seem to see that the "good" parents do not exist.

Adults who hold on to the "good parent" fantasy are surprised every time they're betrayed by the abuser, and shocked when those who abused them in the past continue to abuse them, blame them, and treat them with disrespect. They are surprised that yet again they have done something *to make their parents act that way*. What catches these blinded optimists off guard is the stubborn recurrence of the truth: Their parents are child abusers. They're deniers. They're criminals.

The only way to escape this endless, paralyzing cycle of denial and surprise is to come to terms with the fact that your real parents will never turn into your fantasy parents. The trusted caregivers who abused you were never worthy of trust. You may want to have a relationship with them again, but the relationship must be based in truth. If you want to heal yourself, protect your child, and create the possibility of a healthy future, it's critical to say good-bye to your fantasy mother, fantasy father, fantasy non-protector. They never showed up for you. They never became real. They never existed.

I know this may feel like a painful loss—you will mourn what never could be. But please remember that you are giving your child the loving parenting you have always longed for. The child doesn't need a fantasy parent—he or she has *you*.

ASSIGNMENT 1: Write a Good-bye Letter to Your Fantasy Parents

To help break the spell of the "good parent" fantasy, I'd like you to write a letter to your fantasy mother and your fantasy father. Tell the fantasy version of your abuser good-bye forever, and acknowledge that the fantasy parent(s) could never give you freedom, love, respect, and protection, despite your hopes and wishes.

One of my clients wrote this powerful letter to his fantasy father:

Dear Fantasy Dad:

This is supposed to be a goodbye: a final sendoff to you because you don't exist, never did, and probably never will. The problem is: It's not true. You do exist, just not inside the person where I expect to find you. You don't exist in my father, but you do exist in me.

I keep looking to be respected and listened to by you. I keep looking for unconditional approval from you. I keep wanting you to be different—open, kind, loving. A man who can talk about his feelings, can listen to mine, and doesn't have to try to always know better or know everything. A man who realizes that there is strength in admitting weakness. A father, a friend, a confidant.

I don't want to say goodbye to that dad, because I deserve that dad. So I won't. Oh, I'll say goodbye to that dad in you. I have to, because at least for right now you can't provide it. But if I say goodbye completely, then I will deny that man for myself and for my daughter.

I will let the dad I deserved from you live and grow and thrive in me. I will be all the things for myself and my daughter that you never were. I will never need those things from you again, because I already have them in spades.

So goodbye to you, but hello to me.

SHIFTING YOUR ATTENTION TO YOURSELF

Children who grow up trying to prove their worth to their abusers and pouring their energy into being "good enough" to deserve kindness, care, and respect often become highly sensitive to the opinions, needs, and desires of others. "Maybe they'll love me more if I devote myself to making them happy," the child thinks. The child's sense of all-rightness comes not from within but is always dependent on other people. That means the love the child seeks is always conditional, always based on what he or she does, not who he or she *is*.

Non-protective parents—mothers who don't take their children out of abusive situations, or addicts, for instance—add a staggering burden to the child's already heavy sense of duty. They often turn small sons or daughters into family caretakers, expecting them to assume responsibilities far beyond their ability. As well as coping with abuse, these children stagger under the weight of inappropriate, even dangerous, burdens, and believe their job is to ride to the rescue of the nonfunctional parent. They come to base their sense of goodness on how well they rescue others, and they suffer because they can't possibly measure up.

Mike grew up with parents who were often absent, high, or oblivious to his needs, and it fell to him to care for himself and his neglected sister, even as he was enduring ongoing sexual abuse.

"I feel that my mom put me on a pedestal," he told me. "She made me think that I was going to be famous and rich and go on to unimaginably great things. It made me feel as though I was supposed to be the savior of my entire family. As our lives crumbled and ripped at the seams, it only became more critical that I be the hero in our story."

He took on the responsibility, but it ate away at his sense of self-respect. "I think it was all too much for me," he said. "It wasn't something I truly thought I could accomplish. Even though no one ever said, 'You need to save or fix us,' that's what I heard. My re-action soon became looking for someone to save or fix me. That would be the only way I would ever be able to help my family. But no one ever saved me or fixed me. No one discovered me, and no one died and left me a fortune." He was left waiting, until he de-cided to rescue himself.

The longing for rescue can become entwined with the burden and resentment of feeling that one is valueless if not rescuing others. So I'd like to be very clear: To become the hero in your life, not only must you dismiss the fantasy of the "good parent" or Prince/Princess Charming who will eventually pop onto the scene and hand you a shiny new life, you must also quiet the impulse to prove yourself and your worth by swooping in to meet other people's needs.

Lavish your time, attention, energy, and love on rescuing your child. That's the only way to rewire all the old habits of waiting for a rescue or looking for someone whose needs will take over your life, making you "indispensable" and finally worthy.

You are here to rescue your child. You are here to be *the child's* hero. You must keep putting the child first, now and for the long run.

YOUR CHILD REMEMBERS THE OLD BURDENS; YOU CAN HELP EASE THAT

As Mike thought about the old belief that he needed to be his fam-ily's savior, he realized his child was still trying to take on adult responsibilities. In his morning and evening check-ins, it wasn't uncommon for the child to mention being worried about money or Mike's job. I suggested he do some right-hand/left-hand writing to get to know what adult fears and concerns the child remembered from the past, and to reassure the child that adult Mike was taking care of him, and he could let go of grown-up concerns now.

Here's what the exchange looked like:

Mike:	Hey buddy, how are you today?
MJ (Mike's child):	I'm good. A little tired.
Mike:	I know, we've had some busy weeks. And I know you try and take on a lot of adult things, which is actually what I wanted to talk to you about.
MJ:	What do you mean?
Mike:	I mean that you worry a lot about things you shouldn't. Can you talk about the things you worried about when we were little?
MJ:	Yeah. I worried about mom and dad and Eve. I worried they were going to die or get hurt. I worried that mom was going to leave and never come back. I worried that people were going to make fun of me because I was different and funny looking or say our family was bad.
Mike:	Oh buddy, I'm so sorry that you were so worried. It must have been really scary thinking our family was going to die or that they were going to leave. And I'm so sorry you were worried about being teased and made fun of. You shouldn't have had to think about that. You're so beautiful and handsome and sweet and adorable. You should never feel any less than those things. And if you do I'm here to remind you just how perfect you are.
	Were there other things that you thought were your responsibility or things that worried you?
MJ:	Yeah. I used to worry about the police taking mom and dad away. I worried the police would

give us to strangers. I also worried about not
having food and being embarrassed to ask for
food. I worried about mom and dad fighting and
getting drunk. I worried about him killing us.

Mike: Buddy, you can let go of all those worries now.
You're safe with me and those things can't
happen. I'll never let you go hungry. You never
have to be embarrassed to say you're hungry.
I'm here to do any worrying for both of us. But
honestly, worrying doesn't do anything. So how
about neither of us worries and we just love
each day as it comes? Can you try and do that
with me?

MJ: Yes I will try. But you have to too.

Mike: OK I promise. I love you MJ.

MJ: I love you too.

ASSIGNMENT 2: Talk to Your Child About His or Her "Adult" Worries

As Mike did, use right-hand/left-hand writing to ask if your
child will tell you about what scared him or her in the days
when the abuse was going on. Comfort the child for those
looming old fears, and let the child know the time for worrying is over and that you are there to provide care, protection, and love. Be clear that you will take care of your adult
responsibilities, and the child can be free of them.

GETTING TO KNOW THE HERO IN YOURSELF

Growing up, you were told what you saw, felt, and experienced was
always wrong. But the work we've done so far has shown you your

strength, your wisdom, and your truth. Now I'd like you to explore these aspects of yourself in greater depth. Going through the following exercises, which involve writing a series of letters, is a way to reinforce your connection with the best parts of yourself, and your sense of trust in yourself.

You've come to know your child and the One Who Knows, and now you'll come in contact with parts such as your Inner Hero and the Good Parents inside you. All of us have multiple parts of the self inside, something you've probably intuited and that psychologists have built many sorts of therapy around. A scientist named Marvin Minsky, who studied the brain's neural networks and tried to create machines that could think, described the brain as having 400 different "computers," a whole society of parts that collectively make us who we are.

What I've observed is that in the work we're doing, imagining and connecting with the parts of yourself that you'll meet next, and asking them to share their clear, supportive perceptions, powerfully reinforces the child's sense of confidence and safety. (The healthy adult part of the self can call upon those parts anytime for help and perspective.)

Don't let the number of letters I'm asking you to write—there are six—overwhelm you. You don't have to write them all in a day. Take your time.

You may find some of these letters to be more emotionally draining to write than others. You may simply enjoy writing some of them. You may feel a weight lifting, a sense of relief. You may feel heartened. You may even feel—rightly so—that you are making progress!

The letters can be short. You may write one or two pages for some of them. For others, you may get inspired and write five pages. Write honestly, and stop when you feel complete.

You are writing to explore and define your feelings, and to get to know yourself better. Each letter is an important step toward your new life. Give them your best effort. And don't forget to write them by hand.

ASSIGNMENT 3: Write a Letter to Yourself From Your Inner Hero

In this letter, let your hero introduce him- or herself, and offer his or her help in your efforts to heal. Your hero does have superpowers, particularly the power to cut through re-sistance, denial, fear, and despair. Let this hero take them on and show you what's possible for the two of you.

Here's the letter one client wrote:

Hi. I am your inner hero. I have an enormous amount of strength and courage just for you. I know together we can uncover and face any memories of hurts, beatings, molestations, neglect, and just being fucked and fucked over. You see, I can say these things because I am your inner hero. I am not scared anymore. I have your back!

Together, we will have the life we deserve and cast off all this guilt and shame that is not yours to own anymore. We will give all that back to those it belongs to. It's time for them to take responsibility for hurting you and for not protecting you the way you were meant to be protected. You were a child. You absolutely have the right to be protected and cared for and nurtured.

I can love, if I want, but only those who know how to love you—I mean, really love you, cherish you, and communicate with you. Together, we will face all this stuff and overcome the past, because I know, at the end of it, I will be you!

With love,

Your inner hero

ASSIGNMENT 4: Write Letters to Yourself and Your Child
From the Good Parents Inside

Among the many sources of support inside you are good parents who are available to guide you. These are the good mother (your inner mother) and good father (your inner father) you deserved to have, and whose praise, pride, and support will feed your soul. Ask each of them to write two letters, one to your child and one to the person you are today.

Steven wrote and treasured these two letters from his inner mother:

Dear Little Stevie:

As your loving Mother, I have some wonderful things about you that I must point out. You are a wonderful boy, Stevie, full of love, understanding, and amazing perception. You are an easy friend, loyal and trustworthy. You are a graceful athlete, strong and focused. You possess a sharp and infectious humor. You give of yourself unselfishly, because that is part of who you really are—a loving child of God.

You love plants. Watching flowers open to the sun is something you love very much. And that is okay. I find it lovely. You are very creative, and this is a gift you give fully and freely. Thank you for that. You are special to me, and I will always be a part of your life.

Dear Steven:

You are a beautiful man through and through. You have talent and perceptions that run very, very deep. You are connected to your God, and you can count on your talent. Think of all you have and all you perceive as a bottomless, limitless well, and continue to give it away fully to those who will hear. When you give your love, this is what makes you such a lovely man. You have a handsome spirit. You are beautiful. You are a success, and I know many others who see you feel this way as well. You will continue in your success, and all your dreams will come true, because you are a creator and a vessel of care, love, and affection. People love being around you. Because of this, do not be afraid to shine, my dear son. Shine on, son, and others will shine with you, beyond your wildest dreams.

I love you. I understand you. I admire you. All the painful, difficult, and courageous work you have done on yourself makes you a warrior of the soul. Congratulations!

I hold you both close, as pieces of my heart. I carry you with me forever.

I am your Mother, and I love you.

Love always,

Mom

ASSIGNMENT 5: Write a Letter to Your Body

Part of the task of the hero is to help you appreciate yourself, and see yourself in a new way. Where the abuser saw flaws, weakness, and opportunities to gain an advantage, your inner hero has the ability to see your power, beauty, and amazing capacity for growth and healing. This is the clear vision you will carry into the future.

Look through the hero's eyes and write a letter of appreciation to your body for all it has endured and all the support it continues to give you. Your body has been heroic in itself—you're here, alive today, and this old friend has carried you through your own private hell and war. Rather than putting it down and carrying on the tradition of defaming it, it's important to let your physical being know how important it was, and to praise it for what it did to get you here.

Steven wrote:

I want to thank you, my body, for taking all the abuse others and I have inflicted upon you. Thank you for healing after all the beatings and incest. Thank you for taking all the injuries, the strains, the sprains, the broken bones and the bulging discs and the major surgery on your lower back when you were 23 years old. Thank you for enduring surgery on both hands and for living with the periodic numbness in your legs, arms, and feet that still haunts you. Thank you for living through the emergency appendectomy. Thank you for enduring the chronic pain for so many years. You still get up every morning and face the day accepting the pain as a part of it all.

Thank you for your recovery after a rib was sawed out of you. Thank you for surviving all the drugs and alcohol I put into you over and over again. Thank you for healing my nose after the many times it was broken and subsequently operated on. Thank you for taking all the hard and sometimes brutal hits I gave and was given on all those football fields. Thank you for all the bruises that you healed, the scratches. Thank you for surviving the stress of living the life of an adult abused and incested as a child. Thank you for enduring the hours and hours I was awake and pushing you to the limit strung out on cocaine or tripping out on acid for 2 or 3 days at a time.

Thank you for walking away from those car accidents. Thank you for surviving for days without food. Thank you for not dying from all the promiscuous and unprotected sex I had that was so dangerous to you. Thank you for carrying all that extra weight and then the obsessive exercise to get you back in shape.

Thank you for taking such good care of my mind and for

housing my soul through all the ugliness, selfishness, and abuse you have had to endure.

I am eternally grateful to you.

Love, Little Stevie

Love, Big Steven

ASSIGNMENT 6: Write a Letter to Yourself Stating What Is Right About You

Now I'd like you to look through the eyes of the wisest, most heroic parts of yourself and write a letter to yourself listing and praising your best qualities, and celebrating who you are and what you love. This is a good place to appreciate the progress you've made, the growth you've achieved since you began reclaiming your life from the legacy of abuse. It may feel awkward to do this, to say these good things about yourself. Do it anyway.

Here's what one client wrote:

Dear Me:

I am such a strong person. I feel like I can face anything today that life has in store for me, especially the good stuff. I can love and be loved. I know my job, and I show up every day and do my work at the absolute highest level day after day. I know how to reach out and help people. I am kind. I know how to take care of myself. I have someone who loves me, because I have finally accepted that I am lovable. I love my dogs and cats, and they love me and love being with me. I find it so much easier to make friends day by day.

I like to read and research all kinds of stuff that interests me, because I really love being informed about new events or things I did not know before. I love learning about life and take my lessons and learn from them, without beating the shit out of myself for mistakes I make along the way. I love helping people, but not to the point of exhaustion anymore. I know I can't take care or help anyone unless I take good care of myself and my body. I am a good human being, because I care and I am present and aware today. I am okay with myself.

It can also be effective to make a list you can label "What Is Right With Me," and keep adding to it over time. One of my clients created this list:

WHAT IS RIGHT WITH ME:

- I am a good man.
- I care about others.
- I try to help those in need.
- I work hard to stand up for my beliefs.
- I try not to lie, cheat, or steal.
- I am a hard worker.
- I'm smart.
- I'm well-read.
- I love to teach.
- I'm a good artist and love to paint and draw.
- I express myself well in speech and writing.
- I try to be a good brother and friend.
- I am proud to be a veteran and to have served my country.

ASSIGNMENT 7: Write a Final Good-bye to Your Unrealistic Fantasy of Being Rescued

I know this fantasy is stubborn, so I'd like you to write a letter putting it in the past and describing how you'll move forward, your own hero, without it.

I've never forgotten the letter one of my clients wrote. It's his careful, thoughtful way of acknowledging what it means to be your own hero, knowing the buck stops here, with you:

A Good-bye Letter to the Unrealistic Fantasy

This is a good-bye letter to the me who fantasizes about being able to live, succeed, prosper, create and love . . . without feeling anything, risking or working hard, while abandoning myself, running away and making myself a victim. Good-bye to the me who makes the world responsible for the ease and magnitude of my success, comfort, emotional wellbeing and financial stability.

I am my own keeper and partner, and I'm finally responsible for the containment, love and care of myself and all my pain, fear, discomfort and feelings of abandonment. I am responsible for taking steps to work, create, earn, communicate and foster a safe atmosphere in which I can risk and strive. The old idea that someone else will carry me, will maintain love, consistency, safety and opportunity is an old idea. I must take full responsibility.

To achieve career success I must make all necessary steps along the way. I will tolerate criticism and rejection, which occurs in any creative field in day-to-day life. Waiting for luck or validation or "a break" from the world is a setup for me to be a victim: disappointed, resentful and alone.

I can and should ask for help, but I can never forget that the primary responsibility falls on myself.

Miracles never come in the expected form and I will not try to anticipate them. I will take actions as if miracles never happen—and I will be astounded by their occurrence at all times, all around me.

I am not afraid to take all the necessary little steps. I don't need to take spectacular steps to go to spectacular places.

My own estimable acts create the esteem I so deserve and desire.

ASSIGNMENT 8: Read Your Writing Aloud

When you've finished writing all your letters and your list, read them into your phone or recorder and then play them back. Listen to this record of your resilience, your resources, and the amazing strength and gentleness that is there for your child. This is the voice of your hero. Listen to the recording whenever you need to reconnect with the shining core of yourself.

THIS IS WHAT IT FEELS LIKE TO STOP WAITING AND LET YOUR HERO GO TO WORK

The writing you've just done, these letters of strength and praise you've written from the hero and the good parents inside you, was meant to help you focus on the strength, beauty, and inner power that have always been a part of you. Amanda, whose work with the One Who Knows you saw earlier, took to heart her role as her own hero, and told me at Christmastime one year that she finally understood what it meant to be able to come to her child's rescue any time the child had an unmet need or a heartfelt wish.

"You asked me to have my little girl write a letter to Santa asking for what she wants," Amanda told me excitedly. "I wondered—what was it going to be? Then she wrote two simple sentences—pure, straightforward wishes. I read them and I thought, 'There's no Santa—but *I'm* Santa. And there are two little things I can do for my little girl, gifts from myself to help her feel brave and embrace the world. It sounds cheesy, but sometimes it's the little things that open your eyes.

"She said, 'I want to laugh more, and I want a friend.' And I thought, 'Okay, I get it. This is because I don't have a close girlfriend right now.' But that's not what she was asking for. She wanted *me* to be that friend. And it's interesting, because shortly after, I wrote a letter to myself that said, 'I know you've been going through a hard time, and I want you to know that I love you.' It was the kind of letter you'd like to get from a friend. I'd been wishing I would get a letter like that—so I wrote one. It was huge for me to see that I can do that for myself. I don't have to wait. I can give myself, give my little girl, what she needs. It makes me a better friend, a better mother, a better daughter.

"I'm so much more filled up emotionally now, and every day I see how powerful these little things are, how powerful words are. And when I see that my children or my husband need something, I can go meet that need without resentment, because I've given care to myself, and I can give it out to the world."

Amanda was beaming and joyful as she spoke. No longer waiting for the hero to arrive, she'd found her own way to listen to herself, let her own needs be important—and to soothe the loneliness she'd carried inside her for so long.

12

PAUSE TO FEEL WHERE YOU ARE

Recovering from abuse isn't a simple, linear process with steps you can walk through once and check off the list. This is a process that demands continuing effort, one step at a time, day after day. You're building the loving, hopeful life foundation you never had, using the raw materials of consistency, self-love, fierce honesty, and hope. I'm proud of how far you've come, and I hope you're feeling fired up and empowered by coming in contact with your inner hero. You can call on that hero anytime, and before we move on, I'd like you to give that hero part of yourself a workout by trying some techniques that will pull you steadily along the path to freedom—especially when you feel tired or overwhelmed.

The work we've done up to now has probably revealed layers of emotions and insights into the trouble spots in your life. Each time you do another exercise or sit down to talk to your kid, there's a good chance you'll find more pain to process, more false beliefs to offload, more inner dialogue that no longer serves you. I know you're also discovering wisdom you never knew you had as you become a good parent to your child, helping him or her cope with fears and feelings that sometimes seem to rush out of nowhere. By now, you've seen how significantly your life can improve when you take the time to listen and respond to the child's feelings and desires.

You won't always do it right, and sometimes you'll slip or resist the assignments or feel as if you're just going through the motions. Remember, though, this isn't about "acing the test." (There is no test!) Trial and error is how we learn. Messiness is expected. We work in spurts and stall. We stumble.

Keep giving this work your best. Think often of your child, and give him or her loving care. Pick up the pen and start writing to the child or the One Who Knows whenever you're confused or hurting. Choose any of these genuinely heroic acts, and I promise you'll see positive change.

How are you doing? Let's take stock of what's shifting for you, what still needs attention, and what your next steps should be.

Your next major assignment will be a big one: to tell your abuser(s) what you experienced and how it affected you, and to hold them accountable for their actions. Doing that will require you to draw on all the healing you've done so far and all your devotion to the child inside you. I want you to be ready, and I'll help you decide whether you are.

Before speaking your truth to the abuser(s) and those who didn't protect you, you'll want to strengthen your confidence in yourself as a parent to your kid and as the hero of your own life. You'll want to focus on examining your strong reactions to events and people in your life, and tracing them to their origins in the abuse. You may want to spend more time getting to know the wise person inside you. All this work will ground you in your love and support for the child and create the engulfing sense of safety and security that is the key to claiming your adult power—your ability to put the whole, healthy part of yourself in charge of your life.

You can use the techniques you find here to seek the wisdom and perspective that resides in every part of yourself, both the good and the difficult. I encourage you to dig deep, and to be fearless in facing what you unearth. Remember, fearlessness includes the ability to seek the support of other people as you go, and to build relationships of trust that will speed your growth. Just as recovery in a twelve-step program is an ongoing process, so is your recovery from abuse. As you persist with it, you will shift your relationship with your past until, at last, you no longer feel the heat and anguish of the pain that grew from what happened to you as a child. You'll finally find peace—as an adult in the present.

STRENGTHENING YOUR BELIEF IN YOUR OWN TRUTH

Have you looked at your story lately? I'd like you to spend some time with it before we go on. Find twenty minutes or so in your schedule when you can be alone and uninterrupted, and pull out a photo of your child and the most recent version of your story. Read through it, and make any updates or changes you need to. Then, with the photo as a visceral reminder of how small and vulnerable you were, read your story aloud all the way through, paying attention to the way you feel as you give voice to the instances of abuse and their effects on you. Look into the eyes of the child in that photo and remember what happened to the innocent, hopeful person you once were. Then listen to the original recording you made of yourself reading the descriptions of the abuse you suffered and the pain it brought to your life.

What's changed for you since that original recording? What feelings are coming up as you read and listen today? Are you sad? Furious? Depressed? Outraged for your child? Any and all of these emotions are appropriate, and it's vital to keep feeling and expressing them. Any strong emotions you feel now are expressions of the subterranean pain you've carried around since the time of the abuse, the pain that has been controlling your life from its hiding place in the terrorized world of the child. It may take you many months to sort through the feelings and comfort your child as you come to terms with what happened.

As she healed, Jennifer, the executive assistant, talked about the sense of clarity that began to come from repeatedly looking at what had happened to her, especially in the moments when strong emotions came up. "I wasn't remembering things that were never in my brain before," she said, "but it felt like I was picking out random memories that had never been filed in the right place, and all of a sudden they made sense. I had all these cluster bombs of emotion I'd been keeping hidden, and when they'd surface, I'd think, 'You don't want to open that door because it'll kill you.' But you let one memory out in safety and look at it and realize where the emotion is coming from and how it fits in your past. And you survive. You can see things as an adult, and things start making sense. It's comforting."

Be sure to tune in to your body and to use all the calming, comforting strategies you learned in chapter 5 to ground yourself each time you feel your body tensing into fight/flight responses or encounter one of those "cluster bombs" of emotion. Many people find ongoing relief in the writing exercise you learned earlier: "When you did X to me I felt [this way]. How dare you do X to me!"

Take a minute now to check in with your child with right-hand/left-hand writing to be sure he or she is okay. Ask about anything that came up as you revisited the abuse, and offer any reassurances you need to, to let the child know you are here as a parent and protector, that the abuse is long over, and that the child bears absolutely no responsibility for what happened. Repeat these truths like a mantra or a prayer if you need to. Your child can't hear them often enough.

Never forget: *To absolve the abuser(s) is to blame and abandon your child.* I know you know this, and you're probably wondering if you're stuck in *Groundhog Day* as I repeat it yet again. But layers of sadness and anger and betrayal and hurt surround the abuse you experienced, and every time you hit a new layer, you'll be faced with the temptation to minimize what happened so you can "get on with things." You'll feel the call of your old, familiar ways of numbing yourself, and you'll probably want to check out. Please stay with me, first by calming your body and then by returning to the assignment in front of you. Each facet of the work we've done so far is designed to help you absorb the truth. You *can* be strong for your child, and truly be the hero you've always waited for. Keep the mallet of truth in your hand. Keep whacking away at "It wasn't so bad."

For Jennifer, the process of facing down the feelings and reinforcing the truth was a long one. "After I started doing this work and looking at what happened to me, it took me probably a year to get out of the kind of anger and depression phase," she said. "I had to let myself really acknowledge the pain, and feel everything. At the beginning, I needed to say, 'These people were shit. They did really shitty things to me.' People say you have to move on and can't dwell on the past. But can't we acknowledge it that they were shit, and process it? I spent a long time doing that. I also got a new kind of clarity. What I was feeling wasn't the old, nameless 'What is wrong with me?' depression. I was sad because something happened to me and it was wrong. And I got the feeling that I was achieving something by feeling the sadness. Once I could name it and feel it and live through it, I would never have to reexperience it again. I could leave that 'sadness forever' limbo because I finally connected it to the abuse."

Jennifer, like many of my clients, used yoga as a way of staying connected with her body and learning to stay with the shifting sensations of the present rather than being trapped in the frozen panic of the past when difficult feelings came up. Calming your body is vital when you are swimming in this sea of emotions, and you might want to try it now if you haven't already.

For your child's sake, so you can finally integrate the feeling of what happened and how bad it truly was, you may need to be angry with, and even hate, your parents for a while—and that's okay. You can express your feelings privately—in your journal, in therapy, as you pound a pillow or smash tennis balls against a wall to release your intense emotions. Outrage is appropriate. So is sadness. You'll feel both the child's bewilderment and hurt, and the adult's sense of fury that your child was treated with such cruelty, disrespect, and lack of protection.

But the process doesn't end there. As you examine and feel the emotions surrounding the abuse, they become less immediate. As they become integrated with adult understanding, and are moved from the perpetual present into the past, you can go forward with understanding and compassion for yourself, but without the child's intense distress. In comforting the child, you allow yourself slowly to come into the safety of the present.

Jennifer described that evolution well: "You go to the next step, which is talking to the abusers about the abuse without doing it in anger. You can do that when you understand what happened from an adult point of view. And you're able to see it from an adult point of view once you have processed the feelings. You can't do that if you're still in the kid's world, stuck with emotions you don't know what to do with."

You're ready to confront your abuser(s) with your truth about the past when, without minimizing or rationalizing, you can clearly describe both what happened to you and the repercussions that have affected you ever since. You need to be unshakeable in your understanding of what took place, not wavering, not lying to yourself at the child's expense with "They didn't really mean it," "They had a hard life and didn't know any better," or any other excuse. More than that, you need to have self-protective ways of facing and working with the hot-button emotions hidden in the past so they no longer overtake you.

As people progress, they can tell their stories with compassion for themselves and with a clear sense of cause and effect: The abuser committed harmful acts against the blameless child that affected every aspect of the child's life.

This takes time and practice.

For that reason, I want you to use all the tools I've shared with you so far, and shore up any areas that feel shaky before you go on to the next chapter. I'll help you assess where you are, and suggest some possible paths forward, in the following section.

ARE YOU READY? HERE'S HOW TO TELL

Please put a checkmark beside each of the statements that's true for you today.

☐ I have a good relationship with the child inside me. I've kept my commitments to check in with the child and put his or her welfare first.

☐ The child feels real to me, and I'm learning from our conversations. I like this little person!

☐ I protect my child. That is, I don't put him or her into dangerous situations.

☐ I keep my promises to the child and to myself.

☐ I have put my whole story on paper and read it aloud.

☐ I believe deeply and firmly that my story is true. I believe my child.

☐ I don't minimize what happened to me or downplay its lasting effects. If I find myself doing that, I stop and reaffirm to the child that the abuse was serious, that it was not our fault, and that I hold the abuser(s) 100 percent responsible for what happened.

☐ Every time I feel a strong emotion that's out of proportion to what's happening right now, I go back to the child and trace the feeling to its roots.

☐ I have noticed my emotional reactions are not flying out of the past to surprise me as much as before.

☐ I stayed true to my ninety-day break from contact with my abuser(s) and gained new perspective about them and myself by breaking our old patterns.

☐ I am no longer waiting to be rescued by someone else.

☐ I know what my child loves, and I am rediscovering what I love too. I am bringing more of those elements into my life.

☐ When I'm faced with troubling emotions or big questions in my life, I turn to my child and to the One Who Knows for answers first.

☐ I'm putting myself first more, choosing to do things I enjoy, and believing in myself.

☐ I don't need to rescue anyone. I'm too busy taking care of myself and my child.

☐ I've fallen in love with my child.

Every item on this list is important to your recovery, and if you spot weaknesses, or areas you've overlooked, you need to focus on strengthening them before you go on.

If you feel you need to work on just two or three areas, spend a few weeks paying close attention to what happens if you put more daily energy into them. If you've done more quick skimming of this book than daily work, recommit to action. You are creating new habits, new reactions to old stimulation, and an ever-stronger relationship with the child inside you. The only way to do this is to make a conscious effort, moment by moment. Do your writing assignments and check-ins. Stop to reflect *often*. Take time to plan how you'll care for the child consistently and well. The more consistently you do this, the more your everyday life will reflect your new clarity, purpose, and strength.

You can't think your way to healing. You *feel* your way there, by imagining and empathizing with the child.

Jennifer found that honoring her child's requests for fun opened up parts of herself that she was certain she'd lost. "The turning point for me was really clear," she says. "I remember going to a shoe store to get one pair of shoes. I saw this one pair, a little boot, that I could wear to work. It was 'normal' and wouldn't raise any eyebrows. But there was another pair, strappy and fun. I was getting ready to take photos of them and send them to my husband, so he could help me decide what to get. But then it hit me. I thought, 'Oh my God, I can decide. I can make my own choices and get the things I want for myself.' That was huge.

"I started making my own decisions, realizing what I liked. There was so much I'd forgotten about, whole parts of myself. Anything I thought would be cool, I just started doing it. I'm sewing now, and I started oil painting, took some classes, started tai-chi. All these things.

"It all went back to those little choices I'd begun exploring with my child. 'What do you like? What do you like to do?' When I started asking the question, the answers started coming."

As you become your own authority on you, mapping your child's preferences and then your own, your world begins to fill with what you love. That feeds your soul and gives you a chance to make the kinds of discoveries about yourself that a loving, protective, non-abusive parent might've helped you make. You can move toward what lights you up, and feed your own talents. Hell, you can go ahead and buy the wild shoes without waiting for anyone's permission. You can give this joy to yourself, and it's important to do that as you prepare to share your truth with your abuser(s). Yes, you need to dissolve the lies and build a new relationship rooted in truth. That's essential. But part of your work with the child is to create the life you never got to have. There's joy and beauty and fun in that.

If you are not yet allowing your love for your child to lead you to better self-care and to small, joyful adventures that are opening up your sense of fun at least a little, you're not yet ready to present your truth to your abuser(s). When you face them, I want you to be grounded in a solid core of belief not only in the truth of your story but also in your ability to create everyday happiness for your child in a life that's looking more and more like you.

A RECOMMENDATION: CIRCLE BACK TO THE BEGINNING

This work is cumulative. My clients spend many months with me, in groups that use the same practices repeatedly to develop deep relationships with the child inside and with the truth of their stories. I strongly recommend that if you want to develop your non-victim ways of being, you go back to the beginning of the book, reread the material from the perspective of what you've learned so far, and work through the exercises one more time, focusing on the ones you resist and the ones that attract you most strongly.

I know that may seem unorthodox, and I know you're in a hurry. But please be willing to be slow and thorough. Your child and the One Who Knows are, by themselves, worth significant attention, and the more you learn to take your cues from them, the richer your recovery will become. If you are honestly able to look through the preceding checklist and feel comfortable saying yes to each item, you're ready to move on. And if not, give yourself the opportunity to keep working with the exercises so new ways of being can take hold in your life.

You can also use the techniques that follow to expand the ways in which you look for the truth you can always find inside.

YOU CAN LEARN FROM ANY PART OF YOURSELF

As you've experienced by now, you can turn inward for guidance any time you need to, asking for the child's perspective on where trouble-some feelings originate and what the child inside needs and wants—which often reveals ways you're ignoring core desires and self-care. The wise part of yourself can offer you profound counsel on any issue in your life, and every week in my group sessions, people turn to one another and say, "Sounds like you ought to ask the One Who Knows."

One significant truth your abuser(s) kept from you is that you're filled with wisdom, and the more you look inside for guidance, the more clarity you'll receive.

People have turned to the One Who Knows for insights into questions like:

- Why am I sabotaging myself?
- What do I need to do in my troubling work situation?
- Why do I feel uneasy about what's going on with my partner?
- What's blocking me now?

You can use the same right-hand/left-hand writing you do with the child and the One Who Knows to directly speak to any part of yourself, any person who appears in one of your dreams, or any version of yourself—the baby, the high school student, the person who used to love music but gave it up, or the one who traveled across the country alone at age twenty. The process is the same: Write your question with your dominant hand, and let the reply flow through the nondominant hand. Let the healthy adult part of yourself organize any action you take in response to your new understanding.

I'd like to show you some examples of what my clients have learned by doing this. I'm consistently amazed by how readily people find exactly what they need to know simply by learning to get the most from right hand/left hand.

A QUICK CONVERSATION WITH THE BODY

Like many people who were abused as children, Rose struggled with body-image issues. She grew up calming herself with food, was often critical of her body, and tended to ignore her most basic physical needs. After she mentioned feeling "fat and disgusting" in a group session, she gave herself the assignment of writing to her body to find out how she could improve her relationship with it. Here's what resulted:

Rose: Dear Body, What do you want or need? I am feeling pretty big and disgusting.

Body: I want you to eat better. You also need to sleep more. You will need to set a bedtime and stick to it. No more excuses. It's time to focus on getting healthy physically.

Rose: Thank you Body for being direct with me. I know I struggle with going to bed early. I will make the effort to go to sleep earlier.

Body: Okay, but you need to be committed to make the changes.

Rose: I will start by setting a bedtime. I will go to bed by midnight. I will work on it.

This is not a momentous exchange, yet it moved Rose out of the criticism looping through her head ("I'm fat and disgusting, I'm fat and disgusting") and toward concrete actions that would help her feel better. She had written a letter of appreciation to her body, just as you did earlier. Now she was opening up a new channel of communication to bring its input into the nitty-gritty of everyday life. What concerned her body, she discovered, had nothing to do with food or eating but instead involved the underlying issue of exhaustion, which makes it much harder to maintain both health and perspective. Rose didn't change her schedule immediately, but "enforce a new bedtime" gradually moved up her to-do list, and she began to infuse her life with rest—and to notice more readily when she needed to stop and pay attention when critical voices got louder inside.

LEARNING TO FOLLOW THE CLUES

Rose got into the habit of not only having productive conversations with many parts of herself but also of looking carefully at the information her right-hand/left-hand exchanges produced, so she could ask follow-up questions, the way a journalist or detective might. Often, important clues are buried in the nondominant hand's writing, as was the case when Rose decided to find out more about her feelings of being "not good enough."

> Rose: To the part of me that thinks I am a failure and not good enough. Why do I feel this way? Why are you in my thoughts?
>
> Failure: I hate you bitch. You are fat and ugly. You abandon me you don't give a shit about me. You are a piece of shit bastard.
>
> Rose: Who are you?
>
> Failure: I am the angry side of you. I am the negative pessimistic side. The one that holds you back. I sabotage you every chance I get.
>
> Rose: How can I make you feel better? I don't want you in my life anymore. I want to put you to rest. I have heard you too many times and it hurts me to hear you. I no longer want to hear such unkind words directed

at me. I want all that negativity to be put to rest for
good. I hear you and know that those words are not
true. I am a worthy, kind, gentle woman. I deserve to
be happy and free. I am a wonderful human being. I
am worthy of love and success. I matter. I matter.

You can use questions like Rose's to approach any troublesome
thought. Asking "Who are you and why are you in my thoughts?"
allows that part of yourself to identify itself to you and clarify where
it came from. Let your curiosity lead you, and approach each part of
yourself with respect as you explore the insights it has to offer, and
the purpose it's playing in your life. You might ask:

- Why are you here now?
- Where did you come from?
- Why do you say that?
- What do you mean by X?
- What do you want?
- How can I make you feel better?

You can also challenge the perspective of any part of yourself
that holds you in low regard. Standing up to a negative voice, as
Rose did, is a powerful way to step out of the victim's role.

As we looked at what "failure" had to tell Rose, we kept returning to the words, "You abandon me." Why, Rose wondered, was this
negative, name-calling voice talking about being abandoned? What
was that about?

She went back to ask.

Rose: To the parts I abandon. Which part of me are
you?

Abandoned part: I am the part of you that you abandoned when

you were 7 years old. You buried me with your
dreams and aspirations. You decided that your
dreams and goals were stupid and you were
unworthy.

Rose: What happened at 7 years old that made me
feel this way?

Abandoned part: Lots was going on in your house. Your dad was
always drunk and your mom was in fear. Your
dad and cousin were fucking your aunt. It was
confusing. Your cousin started playing kissing
games. That was the only attention you got. No
one else paid any attention to you. Your sisters
were mean to you. They did not like you. You
were a snitch in their eyes. You were considered lazy because you did not like cleaning or
cooking. You'd rather go outside and work on
the cars. Assemble and disassemble them.

Now we zeroed in on what was going on at Rose's house when she
was seven, and I asked Rose to go back and ask her child for memories of that time. By following the clues that the right-hand/left-hand
writing was producing, we were finally getting to the heart of why
Rose, for all her strengths and successes in life, reflexively labeled
herself a failure instead of celebrating her intelligence and tenacity.
By searching for the cause, we could finally address the real problem.

This is what Rose's conversation with her child looked like:

Rose: Dear Little Rose, the 7-year-old that was abandoned as a kid. Can you tell me what happened?

Little Rose: I was ignored. There was a lot of chaos in the
house. My dad drank a lot and my mom was always
afraid. Maria pretended to be strong and tough.

Pilar was the little one and was protected by Maria.

Rose: Why did you feel alone and abandoned?

LR: I felt alone and abandoned because no one took care of me. I did not matter. It was like I did not belong with this family. I was different. Nobody loved me or cared about what I was feeling.

Rose: I am so sorry that you felt that way. I hear you and can imagine how difficult it must have been for a 7-year-old to be alone to cope with all the chaos around her. I am here with you now to listen, to be with you, to take care of you. I will make sure you are safe and protected. Is there anything else you want to share?

LR: I am frustrated. You say you will take care of me and you don't. I am tired. I am really tired. I keep having weird dreams.

Rose: I know sweetie. I have been trying to go to sleep early and I do feel your restlessness. What do you need me to do so you can get more rest?

LR: I think I need to play more so I am tired when I go to bed. I am too idle.

Rose: OK sweetie. I hear what you are saying and I will start scheduling some play time. Anything else I can do for you?

LR: No that is all.

Rose: OK sweetie. I love you and am there for you.

LR: Love you too!

Rose didn't have an "attitude problem" that she could bully into submission or use "positive thinking" to fix. Pessimism and negative thoughts arose in response to the abuse and neglect she suffered at a very specific time in her life. Now we knew. Now we could work to make the child feel safer, and to reconnect Rose with the optimistic, creative, independent dreamer she'd left behind so many years ago.

These conversations with deeper parts of herself made clear to Rose that lack of physical care was no small thing to her child, and that the child's sense of neglect and abandonment was behind much of the negativity she'd always assumed was just a part of her character. She decided to make a major shift having to do with self-care. "I was a workaholic when I walked in," she told me. "But it's finally sinking in that I can't have a child and be at work for sixteen hours—that is so unkind. Those hours were terrible for me. I would not eat for twelve hours, then I'd go home and binge because I didn't have food for me and Little Rose.

"If I had a child, I would carry water and snacks. So I've started carrying a cooler for us. That was something I would never have done for me, but I can do it for my child. If she is hungry, we eat. If she's tired, we go to bed. I had not learned that in thirty-five years of life, and that is embarrassing. I am a successful career woman, yet I couldn't do basic self-care. Now I carry the cooler everywhere I go. I bring my own food. It's funny when I go see my mom, who's diabetic, because I look like the diabetic—I'm eating every three hours. My mom, even though she's sick, can't do that for herself because she didn't learn it. She couldn't teach me. But Little Rose is teaching me. I'm letting myself care for her, and now I care for myself."

How is your care for your child translating to improved self-care? Are you taking seriously the child's need for food and sleep and safety? When your child asks to rest, or play, do you listen? Do you encourage the child to express his or her uniqueness, rather than conform to what others prefer? If so, you should be seeing changes like Rose's in your life. Remember that when you neglect the child, you continue the abuse. And as long as the child experiences that, it's impossible to come into the present, where healing takes place.

You are deserving and worthy of the best care. Be sure you offer it to the child, and to yourself.

STARTING POINTS FOR REVEALING CONVERSATIONS

Writing to the uneasy parts of yourself, the voices and impulses and feelings you struggle with, can give you invaluable information about what's behind the turmoil, and how it may be connected to your past. You can also use your writing to comfort or celebrate yourself, to declare your intentions—the possibilities are many.

Here are some homework assignments that have opened the door to insight and freedom for many clients over the years. The best assignments come straight out of your life, when you investigate an emotion or look into an issue that's coming up for you at home or work or in your dreams. But these right-hand/left-hand topics, because they focus on such universal issues, always seem to yield valuable insights, and if one catches your eye, let it lead you into a conversation with yourself that may open up new understanding:

- Write a thank-you letter to your sacred body, praising it and telling it how you will treat it with care and respect.
- Write to money. If you feel unworthy of having it, ask why.
- Write to men and to women. Tell them how you feel about them and the way they behave, and see what they have to say to you. Express your love, hate, and complicated feelings— everything you've always wanted to say but have been afraid to. For this exercise alone, use only your dominant hand.
- Write to sexuality, especially if you fear it.
- Write to love, telling it your hopes and fears and asking about how it sees you.
- Write to yourself in utero, welcoming the baby you were into the world and asking what that baby perceives.

I'd like to share a couple of Mike's assignments to give you an idea of the power of this writing. What's important, always, is not any sort of literary quality. The value is in the emotional truth of the words and the courage it takes to put that truth on paper.

EXAMPLE: A CONVERSATION WITH SEXUALITY

Mike struggled with his attraction to men outside his partnership and worked determinedly to figure out what was driving the impulses that threatened to jeopardize his relationship with the love of his life. He faced the issue directly in this right-hand/left-hand exchange:

> **Mike:** Hi sexuality can we talk?
>
> **Sexuality:** Sure. What do you want to talk about?
>
> **Mike:** I'm not exactly sure. Probably the fact that I'm terrified of you.
>
> **Sexuality:** I know. It's not your fault. You have a long history.
>
> **Mike:** I know. But it's time I faced my fear with you. I'm terrified that you will always ruin my life. I feel that you only want to sabotage all that's good and you always strike when I'm weakest.
>
> **Sexuality:** I know you don't trust me. But you don't even know me. You link me with old childhood molestation, shame, secrets, betrayal, and AIDS. But me, the real me is pure and natural and there should be no shame attached.
>
> **Mike:** If that's so then why do you want to live out fantasies and fulfill lusts that will only bring heartache to us and the people we love?
>
> **Sexuality:** I don't. Those are old thoughts, old ideas. You turn to them because you're afraid to get to know me. You choose to stick to what you know. But freedom lies in the unknown.

Mike: How can I make those old ideas, those old feelings
and fantasies go away?

Sexuality: You open yourself to new ones. You let go of the
shame and you embrace me.

Mike: I desperately want to embrace you, to know you. I
want to be better. I want to feel normal.

Sexuality: Then let go. Stop clinging to the past. You'll be just
fine.

As a result of this conversation, Mike decided to open himself to the new by sharing his sexual fantasies with his partner, and
asking his partner to reciprocate, a conversation that had always
seemed too risky—even with the person he loved most. But as he
found himself delaying and delaying about bringing up the subject,
he realized he first needed to find out what was behind his fears. He
did this, too, in right-hand/left-hand writing. The result surprised
and emboldened him:

Mike: Hello fear. I'd like to talk with you about this wall
you're putting up. Can you tell me why you're stopping me from talking to John about sex and about
our fantasies?

Fear: Because you're afraid to be judged. You're afraid
he will think he's not enough and then things will
change.

Mike: I understand that fear, but we've overcome much bigger things in this life, so why is this so much scarier?

Fear: Because you're afraid to lose him. You're already
backing away emotionally so you won't get hurt. But
if you don't face this, the pain will come regardless.

Mike: Well then how can I get over this fear and just talk
to him about it?

Fear: You have to trust. Trust that he loves you and trust that you'll be ok no matter what.

The wisdom that comes from your core, rather than the outside, has a power and authority that another person's advice cannot. Mike, hearing his fears telling him to trust his partner's love, decided to do that. He took a chance on intimacy, and that's what he got in return.

Each time you find yourself meeting inner resistance to an action you know you want to take, or feel taunted by a part of yourself that seems to be undermining you, use right hand/left hand to understand what's going on, layer by layer. Keep asking for help and insights, and those insights will come.

Example: Expressing Love to the Baby You Were

I often ask people in my groups to write to the youngest version of themselves, the child/spirit they were before they were born. You can show love to yourself at any age, but it's often revealing and moving to speak to yourself in utero. Mike used the opportunity to reassure the child inside that he was ever and always loved:

Mike: Hello my beautiful baby. Can you tell me what it's like where you're at?

The baby: It's dark and warm. I hear voices. They're loud. I don't want to leave. I'm sad because I know what's coming. I'm going to be scared and alone.

Mike: My poor baby. Don't be sad. You have me now and you're never going to be alone again. When you're sad, I'll hold you, and no matter what's going on I'll always love you. You're perfect and I'm here to protect you.

Baby: I know. But you just got here. It's been dark for a long time. I miss being close to her.

Mike: I know, and it's okay to feel that way. But I'm here now and I am your good father and your good mother.

Baby: I don't want to think about being born.

Mike: Why not?

Baby: Because I don't. It doesn't make me feel happy.

Mike: Okay, I understand. I won't make you. But I'm here for you. I'm going to love you and care for you and keep you safe. This time, you're going to get all the love and care you deserve. You're safe with me now. I love you.

One thing you'll notice about all the examples we've seen is that they're direct, honest, and courageous in laying out their emotions, unafraid of feeling or asking questions. This is the voice of the centered, curious adult, the sound of the hero in action. Work with the parts of yourself, especially your child and the One Who Knows, until you see the same directness and courage in your exercises.

Recovery is a *process*. As Bill, the accountant, put it: "'Talk to the child. Talk to the One Who Knows.' Sometimes it feels too simple. Too annoying. Too pedestrian. Until you do it one more time and experience what it feels like to pay attention to what's happening inside you. What I keep learning is that the kid always knows how he feels, and if I keep going to the kid, I find out what *I* feel. I'm not used to feeling. I'm used to *evaluating* how I feel. But it keeps getting easier. I get there faster and faster. And I'm doing it in the middle of whatever comes up. That's what's changing my life."

Take as much time as you need to feel these changes taking hold. Use the checklist in this chapter as a measure of your progress. And when you feel ready, proceed.

13

CAREFRONTATION

You're about to take the step that will move you the furthest and fastest from victim to empowered adult: confronting your abuser(s) with the truth of what they did to you and how it affected your life.

I call this confrontation a carefrontation to emphasize that it is an act of caring for yourself and for your kid. This is the most loving, healing, and affirming gift you can give your child.

I know the idea of a confrontation may sound aggressive to you, but a *carefrontation* is not. The point is not to threaten your abuser(s), start a fight, or make things worse for everyone. Your goal is to free yourself from the tangle of secrets and lies the family has spun around the abuse—and to give your abuser(s) a second chance to be the loving, compassionate people they should have been when you were young.

You can't do this by speaking the truth alone in your room. You must tell it to those who abused you, those who aided them or ignored their actions, and those in your life who deny the abuse took place. You must also carefront anyone with whom you are in a relationship based on lies or a denial of the abuse.

It's vital to share your truth with those who failed to protect you and allowed the abuse to continue. Remember: Those who did nothing were negligent, at the very least, and are culpable for that negligence. You probably resent them for their part in the abuse, and that resentment is a barrier standing between you and any possibility of closeness that is real, not faked.

I know the prospect of finally telling your abuser(s) what you experienced as a child can seem terrifying to consider, especially when you've let their lies sit unchallenged for years. You may worry you'll destroy your relationship with them or that you shouldn't jeopardize the fragile peace. But the peace has been a lie too, and the relationship has been toxic. Its corrosive fictions have created distance, not intimacy, and by denying the reality of the abuse you suffered, the whole act of "keeping the peace" has long betrayed you and your child, and has left you stuck with a lifetime of blame, shame, and guilt for what happened to you. All that belongs to the abuser(s), not to you. And when you return it to the abuser(s) during the carefrontation, you will feel an enormous burden lift.

You are perfectly sane for "stirring things up" and "opening Pandora's box" by choosing to end the lies. Your truth will not destroy the family. The abuser destroyed the family. A carefrontation will offer everyone an opening for healing that no one else has been strong enough to create. In creating a bridge of truth, and asking your abuser(s) and non-protector(s) to cross it to be with you, you'll be giving them a chance to step up and transform your relationship into one built on honesty and respect. Carefronting them frees you of the burden of pretending your relationship with them is good and everything is fine as it is. *Nothing can be okay as long as the truth remains hidden.*

Whether they accept the opportunity for change or battle to maintain the status quo, *you* can begin anew, knowing who is willing to stand with you, who is willing to listen to your feelings, and who is willing to show up for you now.

I've helped hundreds of people find the courage to carefront their abusers. I'll show you exactly how to prepare and then guide you through the meeting and what comes next. Nervousness and hesitation are natural when you're doing something this new—shifting the balance of power between you and the abuser(s) that's been in place for a lifetime. But if you feel panicked and notice your fight/flight responses kicking in strongly as I describe this, it's a sign that your child still feels powerless and unprotected and there's more soothing and listening to do. If you find you're feeling swamped by strong emotions, please go back to the previous chapter and work with the exercises a little longer, expanding your ability to calm your body and make your child feel safe and understood. Then, when you're ready, come back and take on this vital last task.

Carefrontation is a turning point. It's your opportunity to face your abuser(s) as a fully empowered adult protecting your child. When you take this step, you will demonstrate decisively to the child that the people who abused you or did not protect you are no longer a threat. You have slowly and steadily brought the child's hidden fears and memories to the surface, absorbed them, and let the whole of you know that the abuse is in the past. Now, it's time to bring your truth to the abuser(s).

Simply confronting them with what they did, adult-to-adult, will change you. No matter what the outcome, no matter how the abuser(s) respond, you are the victor when the child sees and hears you holding the abuser(s) accountable. With your actions, you're saying to that child: "I know what happened to you. I'm taking care of it. I'm taking the responsibility off your shoulders and putting it where it's always belonged."

Study your photo of the child, and connect with that amazing being whom you've come to know and nurture and love. You've both come so far. Don't rob that child of this chance to be completely free.

None of us can change the past, but we *can* create better tomor-
rows. Remember that when the truth is out in the open, healing
is there for all who embrace it. You will heal. Your child will heal.
And your family can too—if it chooses to stand with you.

THESE NINE STEPS WILL TAKE YOU THROUGH THE CAREFRONTATION

In your carefrontation, you'll read your abuser(s) your story and ask
them to take full responsibility for abusing you or failing to protect
you. You'll ask them to tell you that you were an innocent child,
and in no way responsible for what happened.

People who want to be good parents, and decent human beings,
will take this opportunity to apologize and make things right. Will
the people who hurt you be big enough to do that? You have no way
of knowing, but whatever the response, you'll come away with more
clarity than you've ever had about the kind of relationship that is
possible between you, and what they're willing to do now to support
your healing.

The whole process may take just fifteen or twenty minutes, but
this is the culmination of the work we've done, and I want you to
walk in feeling prepared, solid in yourself, and with an unshakeable
belief in your story. I'd like you to spend the necessary time attending to the details that will ensure you're ready.

STEP ONE: REWRITE YOUR STORY AS
CLEARLY AND CONCISELY AS POSSIBLE

I hope you've written your story at least a couple times by now. Over
time you've been adding details, clarifying what's most important,
and capturing not only the facts but also the emotional impact of
what happened. Please write your story again now as a letter to your
abuser or abusers that makes clear to them what you went through.

Start with the facts of the abuse—sexual, physical, emotional—and also describe any neglect. Then describe how the abuse affected you and your life. Next, describe your recovery and the work you've put toward it, which may include work with psychotherapists or sponsors. In all this, be truthful and to-the-point.

You should be able to do this calmly and without despair, knowing clearly, because of your work with the child, that your life doesn't end with the story of your abuse. Everything you've done for your child has given you a new beginning. That's part of your story too.

Read the letter aloud to your therapist or therapy group, or to a trusted friend. Ask for feedback that can help you gauge whether it is clear and emotionally connected. You may wind up writing several drafts. You will read the final draft to your abuser(s), so once you've refined your story, add two additional final elements:

- An introduction that lays down the ground rules and format for the carefrontation. Say something like: "[Name], thank you for coming today. This is a big step in my recovery. I've been doing a lot of work on myself, and today I want to share with you what happened to me when I was a child and how that has affected me ever since. I need you to listen to me without interrupting. Please respect my wishes and let me read to the end of the letter to you before you say anything."

- A closing statement about what you need from your abuser(s) now, so the relationship can go forward—if you want it to. You might say something like: "I know there's nothing you can do about the past. If you want to make things right in the present, I need you to acknowledge what happened, take responsibility for the abuse, and apologize to me for what you did [or for not protecting me]. I also need you to tell me that what happened was not my fault, that you were the adult, and that you were supposed to protect me. If you're willing to do that, we can have a relationship based in truth and trust.

My client Emily wrote this clear, effective letter to her mother:

Dear Mom:

Thank you for showing up for me today. Sharing this with you is a huge step in my journey toward shedding the shame that was not mine in the first place and becoming the woman I was meant to be. What I am going to share with you is the story of how I was abused, how that abuse impacted me, and my recovery. Please listen to me without interrupting. You can respond when I've finished reading this letter.

Abuse. I suffered from emotional abuse, sexual abuse, and neglect.

Emotional. You told me that I was responsible for being your "friend," earning my keep, and paying you back for the sacrifices you made for me. Specifically, you demanded that I include you in my relationships, run interference for you in your relationships—both personal and professional—put your needs above mine, talk to you about adult issues such as your childhood and relationships, shoplift for you, clean up after you, and do errands for you.

You relied on grandma and grandpa to take care of me and then told me I betrayed you by having a relationship with them.

In many ways, I was the collateral damage of your illness. You screamed profanities and hit yourself in wild tantrums that lasted hours. You drove recklessly, claiming you didn't care if you killed us. You threatened suicide.

You projected your fear, shame, self-loathing, and anxiety onto me.

You made my special moments about you. You cried at my college graduation because no one was there to support you. You called me at the hospital when my first daughter was born to complain that no one was congratulating you on being a grandmother.

You taught me that I had to be thin to be lovable.

Sexual Abuse. When I was about 8 years old, one night after a trip to Disneyland, your boyfriend molested me in your bed. The next morning, you said I had betrayed you, I was a bad friend, and you were not going to give me a special Winnie the Pooh you had gotten for me. I felt ashamed, guilty, and alone.

Around the same age, I spent my mornings at the oceanography lab. The oceanography teacher fondled me while I looked at the fish. I felt ashamed and alone. After my car accident, you sent me to physical therapy. The therapist fondled my breasts. I felt confused and didn't want to confront it, so I pretended to be asleep.

Grandpa "bumped into" my breasts until you confronted him about having done it to you.

Neglect. You didn't teach me basic self-care habits like regular teeth brushing, face washing, bathing, etc. You taught me to eat at other people's houses, steal food, and be thin at any cost.

Effects. I felt confused, anxious, inadequate, and undeserving.

I thought I had to be constantly working to avoid some impending doom.

I thought everyone else's needs were more important than my own.

I felt it was shameful not to be perfect.

I felt devastated by mistakes and paralyzed by the fear of making them.

I obsessed about my weight: compulsively eating, dieting, counting calories, and judging myself based on the number on the scale.

I was a martyr in my relationships.

I didn't have intimate relationships.

I felt different and alone.

I shoplifted compulsively.

I saved money compulsively.

Recovery. I have been in therapy with Arlene, and I am taking better care of myself than I ever have. I feel entitled to have fun, make mistakes, feel my feelings, and say "No." I am learning to be kind to myself. I am proud of my hard work and of the wife, mother, friend, and person who I am.

I know you can do nothing about the past. If you want to make it right, what I need from you is for you to acknowledge what happened and take responsibility for your abusive actions by apologizing.

At that point, we have a chance to start a relationship based in truth and honesty.

I'm not sure what the next chapter is for us. That depends on you. What I do know is that I will move forward in my life in a way that is kind and gentle to myself first.

REVISE UNTIL THE LETTER IS CLEAR

Rose brought one of her letters to our therapy group several times, adding to it and refining until it felt right. She'd focused on her parents' abuse in her earlier years of therapy, and she felt little apprehension about telling them how their drinking, physical abuse, and lack of protectiveness had affected her. Ever since she'd taken her ninety-day break from them, she had kept firm boundaries in place and taken care of herself when they were together. But she was extremely nervous about carefronting her cousin Richard, who had sexually abused her. The sexual abuse had never been acknowledged in her family, and she was particularly concerned about how her cousin would respond.

Though she had never questioned her memories of what had happened, as she approached the carefrontation, she began to feel shaky. She worried about what it would mean to bring that truth into the open, so we worked to calm her fears—and keep them out of the letter.

In one early draft, she listed memories as though she were thinking out loud, including qualifiers like "I vaguely remember" and "I can't remember what the result was." She never told her cousin why she was describing the abuse, or said specifically how she wanted him to respond:

Richard,

I am writing to you because I would like to tell you that I know that when I was a young child you touched me inappropriately. I was a young girl starved for love and affection. I wanted the same attention my sister Maria was getting. Men were generally interested in Maria since she was older and had developed physically well. I invited any attention that I could get from anyone. You were inappropriate with me and with Maria and my Tia Mara. I remember how once I walked into the room and you were having sex with my Tia Mara. I was confused and startled because I thought it was not ok that you were having sex with her.

I vaguely remember incidents that we had. I know that you kissed me and fondled me when I was a child. I remember when one time you were going to run an errand and I enthusiastically volunteered to go with you. You drove down Van Nuys Blvd. by the DMV. I was in the back seat and you pulled over to the side of the road. You stretched your hand backwards to reach the back seat where I was laying down. I knew what was going to happen. You placed your hands inside my pants and started rubbing my vagina. It felt good to get attention in affection. I went numb and can't remember what the result was . . .

If you find yourself getting lost in the details at the expense of making absolutely clear to the abuser(s) why you are telling your story, simplify your letter until it is a calm statement of what happened and what you want from them. Strip away the qualifiers and doubts and lay out what you and your child know is true.

This is part of Rose's final letter. Notice how clear and direct it has become:

Richard,

I am writing to you today because I want to acknowledge what you did to me when I was a little girl. You sexually abused me. It took me a long time to realize that what you did to me was wrong. I remember that you would touch my vagina with your fingers. I also remember playing kissing games with you. Today I realize that this was inappropriate and it affected me more than I was willing to admit. For many years I was afraid that someone would find out and think it was my fault. I was afraid my dad would find out and kill you. I felt so much shame because I thought I provoked it.

Now I know that it was not my fault and that it was not okay. I was a child and you were an adult. You took advantage of my young age and I trusted you. I want to speak my truth and this is it. You sexually abused me and it hurt me.

What I need from you is an apology that you take responsibility for this . . .

Use Rose's final letter, and Emily's, as models for the directness and clarity your letter needs to have.

STEP TWO: SET A DATE FOR THE CAREFRONTATION

When you've finished your letter, set a target date for the carefrontation. Give yourself three to four weeks to ensure you're ready, and to work with any fears and doubts that come up. Put the date in your calendar, and tell the key people in your support system.

Setting a target date will make the carefrontation very real to you, and you may find yourself slipping temporarily from the adult role you've so carefully worked to strengthen. As you move toward taking all your self-knowledge and understanding of the abuse out of your private realm and sharing it with the abuser(s), you may be surprised to see that you're visualizing the carefrontation from the point of view of your child, who is terrified of standing up to them. *You're not a helpless child any longer.* You must hold fast to your most powerful self, and see your abuser(s) through the eyes of the adult you are today, not that scared, injured child. That's the only way to take your power back.

Here are eight telltale signs that you're slipping into the child's role:

- You feel conflicted again about holding the abuser responsible for what happened.
- You find yourself feeling sorry for the abuser(s), not the child. (*You* were the victim, not them!)
- You have trouble connecting with your hard-won clarity, and you feel confused.
- You vacillate between blaming them and blaming yourself.
- You find yourself making excuses for them.
- You tell yourself it's fine to keep things the way they are.
- You feel, once more, like a victim of your secrets.
- You feel yourself regressing into a helpless person who can't do anything to change this relationship.

The victim stance is as familiar as an old pair of pajamas, and it may feel comfortable, even "inevitable," to slide into it again. But stay true to your child and *don't do it*. This is not the time to dump the child and side with the abuser(s). The rise of these old doubts and fears is not a "sign" that you're headed for trouble and need to turn back. It's a sign that you've reached the last test of your commitment to the child and you're getting close to being on the other side.

You may be nervous. But you've proven you're a hero, and a hero feels the fear and takes action anyway. You know how to calm your body, and your child. Do that first. Then visualize yourself as the powerful adult who steps between your child and the abuser and says, "No more!" See yourself as the one who is there—body, voice, and soul—to defend that child and undo the damage of the past. You may be afraid to do this for yourself, but you *must* do it for the child.

You will be the first person who has ever taken on the abuser(s) and their colluder(s) and stood up for the innocent victim you were.

STEP THREE: STAY IN CLOSE TOUCH WITH YOUR CHILD AS THE CAREFRONTATION APPROACHES

The best way to strengthen your adult identity as you prepare for the carefrontation is to tend your child carefully. Pay attention to the child's fears, impressions, and concerns. Comfort and reassure the child, explaining that you will protect him or her as you speak to the abuser(s).

Rose wrote to her child daily in the weeks before the carefrontation with her cousin, and noticed that for the first time, her child feared that she wouldn't—or worse, shouldn't—be believed:

> Rose: Dear Little Rose, How are you feeling about calling Richard and having the carefrontation?

Little Rose: I feel scared. I am afraid that he is going to deny it.
He may think I am lying. What if I made it up?

Rose: Sweetie you did not make up what you feel. It
is real. If nothing happened between you and
Richard you would not have the feelings of anger,
shame and feel anxious. I know it is uncomfortable
to think of confronting him. I will be doing the
carefrontation and will make sure you are safe and
protected. I believe you sweetie.

Little Rose: I am scared.

Rose: I can understand you being scared sweetie. You are
not alone. I am there with you. I love you and I am
here just for you.

Little Rose: Okay I love you too.

Rose: Is there anything you would like me to tell him?

Little Rose: Yes, that he hurt me.

Rose: Okay sweetie I will tell him. We will be fine
sweetie. Anything else I can do for you?

Little Rose: No, that is all.

As the day neared, Little Rose continued to express her fear,
and Rose continued to show up as a strong, loving adult, calming
and reassuring her:

Rose: Dear Little Rose, How are you feeling? Is there
anything I can do for you?

Little Rose: No I am scared. What if he denies it or says it's not
true?

Rose: Sweetie, it does not matter what he thinks or says.
What matters is that you get to speak your truth
and that we know it's true and we believe ourselves.
I am here to protect and love you.

Little Rose: I know you love me and that makes me feel better. I love you too.

Rose: I am proud of you sweetie! I love you very much.

The more you have regular conversations with the child, and keep the child at the front of your mind, the less possible it becomes to betray or abandon him or her for the sake of "keeping peace" with the abusers.

It has taken a tremendous amount of courage to come this far. Don't give up. Don't abandon yourself now. If you don't carefront your abuser(s), you will stay stuck in helplessness, and the past will continue to control you. This is the point where true heroes don't stop. On the other side of the fear is freedom. You're armed with the truth, and that's all you need. People who don't want to hear and tell the truth are those who live in lies. Be strong. Come through for your child.

STEP FOUR: DECIDE WHAT KIND OF CAREFRONTATION YOU WANT TO HAVE

There are three ways to carefront your abuser(s) and non-protector(s):

1. In person. It is ideal to look the other person in the eye and speak to him or her as an adult, not a child. A face-to-face meeting may be scary, but it is extremely powerful to have the physical experience of confronting those who hurt you.

    I strongly suggest you choose an in-person carefrontation as long as you don't think you'd be putting yourself in physical danger.

2. By phone. If the abuser or non-protector is far away, unwilling or unable to meet you, or poses a physical threat, you can call and read your letter. You'll still get the benefit

of speaking your truth, being heard, and learning from the other person's response.

3. By proxy. It may not be possible or reasonable for you to meet or call. You may believe the other person will not listen or let you finish. The other person may be ill, or dead. In such cases, put a photo of the abuser or non-protector in front of you and arrange to read your letter aloud in the presence of someone you trust. It can be cathartic and freeing to carry your letter to an abuser's grave and to read it there if you're able to go. You may also want to read the letter and then burn it.

No matter what form the carefrontation takes, telling your truth is life-changing. Carefrontation is liberation!

STEP FIVE: PUT YOUR SUPPORT STRUCTURE IN PLACE

You'll want to arrange separate carefrontations for each abuser or non-protector. If you are working with a therapist, arrange to have any meeting with the abuser(s) in the therapist's office, with the therapist present. It's important that any therapist you enlist is clear about the goals of the carefrontation and that you have shared all the work leading up to it in this book. If you plan to meet your abuser(s) without the support of a therapist, arrange to do it in a safe, neutral location where you feel comfortable and can easily leave or ask the abuser(s) to leave if you need to. Ask your spouse, partner, sponsor, or a trusted friend to accompany you.

If you're having the conversation by phone, arrange to bookend the call by speaking to a trusted person before and after.

If you're doing the carefrontation by proxy, plan to meet a trusted person who will listen to you read your letter aloud.

Block out time after the carefrontation to talk with a therapist or friend about what happened, and to communicate with your child. Please don't set up a carefrontation without support. You don't have to do this alone.

STEP SIX: MAKE A DATE WITH THE ABUSER OR NON-PROTECTOR

Contact the person to arrange a time for your meeting or call. You can say something like, "I'd like to set up a time to tell you what's been going on with me. It would mean a lot to me to have this conversation with you." If you're meeting in person, let the person know the place you've chosen.

STEP SEVEN: BE VERY CLEAR THAT YOU'RE DOING THIS TO CHANGE YOURSELF, NOT THEM

In a carefrontation, you're not waiting for the abuser(s) or non-protector(s) to answer you, agree with you, or feel sorry for you. Your only job is to let them know what happened to you, tell them that it hurt you and that it wasn't okay, and hand them back every bit of the guilt, shame, and responsibility you've carried about the abuse.

Today, your happiness doesn't depend on their approval the way it did when you identified only with the hurt child inside. The adult you have become does not need to long for others' permission to feel happy, valued, and whole. You *know* you are valuable. You *know* you are worthy. You know how precious and perfect your child is. You know your truth. Now you are strengthening your relationship with your own power, and expressing that power by telling that truth.

You have taken many small steps toward building your adult authority and agency, gaining confidence, and discovering who you are and how truly heroic you can be. The work you've done in this book so far is proof that you can change yourself—that you can grow and become stronger—by taking one step at a time.

You have proven that you can break through the fears that have limited you. Now you have the courage to blossom and become the adult you were meant to be.

I know your fear may be strong. But I believe you will walk through it to save your life.

Go for it! You are ready.

STEP EIGHT: CAREFRONT YOUR ABUSER(S) AND THOSE WHO DID NOT PROTECT YOU

On the day of the carefrontation, reread your letter and write to your child one more time to say you'll be his or her champion when you face the abuser(s). Give yourself plenty of time to get to the meeting, and if you're feeling shaky, soak in the encouragement of the people who are supporting you.

When you are ready to read your letter, ask your abuser(s) or non-protector(s) to sit across from you, if you're in the same room. Pause after you read the ground rules asking that your listener(s) let you finish without interrupting. When they agree, continue, re-membering to breathe. Don't feel pressured to rush through this. It's okay if you cry. You may experience strong feelings, but don't stop. Keep going. Read the letter slowly and clearly, all the way to the end.

As you finish, silently congratulate yourself. You have just com-pleted the most difficult part of the carefrontation. You've finally placed your truth in front of your abuser(s), and you have spoken for your child. Be proud of yourself. You have come a very long way.

At this point, the abuser(s) will respond, if you're together or on the phone. You've offered them an opportunity to be here for you now, to take responsibility for failing to protect you, and to rebuild a relationship with you that has the possibility of bringing you closer than you've ever been. Now you'll see their true colors.

You have been working hard to get at the truth, but your abuser(s) may still be protecting themselves with denial. Rather than taking responsibility for the abuse, they may try to make excuses or focus on tiny details to avoid looking at the big picture. They may tell you, you are misremembering or flat-out wrong. They may dispute your facts. They may say you made up everything in the letter, that you're trying to destroy the family, or that while you may believe everything you read to them, you're crazy. They may even say you've staged the carefrontation to hurt them.

Responses like that are extremely difficult to bear, but they're not unusual. As you listen, you'll discover what's more important to the abuser(s) and non-protector(s)—the relationship with you or protecting themselves with the lies. You may not like what you hear, but you're on a fact-finding mission, so don't cut them off by jumping in to defend yourself right away. Simply listen.

It's important not to get dragged into disputes over every detail and argue over the dates and times of every memory. What matters is the truth of your experience, the accumulation of wounds and scars that you carry inside. Hearing what you experienced, and the reality of how they hurt you, may put the abuser(s) on the offensive. One easy way of doing that is to attack your credibility by debating whether something happened at three a.m. or four a.m., and whether it was on a Friday or a Saturday, or the 10th or the 11th of a particular month. That's a diversion. This is not a court of law, and those details don't matter. *You* matter. Your experience matters. Your suffering matters. No one can dismiss that by arguing that when you were a child, you should have made a note of the dates and times of your abuse so people would believe you later.

If your abuser(s) get argumentative, simply repeat something like:

- I stand by what I said in my letter.
- I've told you what I remember, and I stand by it.
- It happened. Mom, it happened.

If they say, "Why didn't you tell me then?" say, "Because I was a child, and I was too afraid."

No matter what their excuses, you cannot accept or validate them. They might say, "Well, I didn't know it was happening" or "I thought something else was going on" or "I thought everything was okay. You seemed happy." But there are no excuses.

If the abuser(s) go on and on with rationalizations, you need to intervene and say, "Those are excuses. Your job was to protect me, and you failed." Their reasons don't matter. They failed at their most important job.

Close by repeating what you said in the letter: "I know we can't change the past, but we can make a better future. What I need from you is for you to take responsibility for not protecting me [or for abusing me]."

You, as a child, were not responsible for your own well-being and protection. That was the adults' duty, and they hurt you immeasurably by violating that sacred trust. Ask them to tell you that the abuse was not your fault. You were just a child. It was their responsibility to keep you safe and care for you.

It is life-changing to take this stand for your child. And it is transformative to hear the abuser(s) tell you and the child, "I take full responsibility for what happened to you. It was not your fault."

I have witnessed this process many times and have seen the enormous amount of healing that comes from those words when an abuser or non-protector is willing to speak them. They go right to the heart of the wounded child. But whether or not your abuser(s) say them, *you* have protected the child. Whether or not they wanted to take responsibility, you left it with them. And that makes all the difference.

STOP "SHIELDING" THOSE WHO DIDN'T PROTECT YOU

Mike's mother had let him suffer at the hands of his father and others because she couldn't summon the will and courage to protect her own kids. It was second nature for Mike to let her off the hook for that because she had been addicted and needy, and he was accustomed to seeing both of them as victims. But for the sake of his child, he set up a carefrontation with his mom, and with her help, he finally stopped making excuses for her.

"My biggest breakthrough in the carefrontation was realizing just how closed off I was from my mom," he told me. "I always said I was a mama's boy, and I walked in thinking our relationship was perfect. But in fact, when I had her in there with me, I realized I couldn't be honest with her. I had too much resentment, too much anger. The only way to have a true, genuine relationship was for me to clear the air. She didn't protect me when I was little, and I knew I couldn't keep pretending that was okay. I had to let her own it, take it on, and not worry about how or whether she could handle it.

"It was so hard for me. I said what I had planned to say, but almost immediately I tried to soften it to make it easier for her. I started to go, 'I know things were tough for you.' But she's been doing a lot of work on herself too, and she made me stop. She said, 'Mike, you were a little boy and I let terrible things happen to you. It was my fault, not yours. Yes, things were hard for me, but that is no excuse. I can't let you make excuses for me.'

"And finally, I said, 'You're right. There's no excuse. I needed you to protect me, and you didn't. It hurt me so much.' That was the first truly honest thing I had said to her in years, and it was a huge relief. Since I let her take on the responsibility for what happened, we've been able to stop pretending to each other and become a real mother and a son. It's taken time, but she knows who I am now. She knows how I really feel. There's no more big lie between us. The feeling of that is—I couldn't even put a price tag on it."

The relationship you've always wanted with your parents can't ever exist if you continue to live the lie. In the best-case scenario, you'll find yourself with an authentic, even close relationship when you're honest with them about what you experienced. Will that happen for you? The only way to find out is to try.

YOUR CHILD WINS NO MATTER WHAT

You have overcome years of fear and anxiety to become the hero your child needs, and you may have more expectations than you're willing to acknowledge about how the carefrontation will go. You may be bracing yourself for an angry denial at the same time you fantasize about a teary reunion or a reconciliation.

It's possible you'll be met with deafening silence, or an insistent refusal to budge from the story they've always told.

No matter what you get, you've told your truth and you have rescued your child. Congratulations.

You've chosen truth and clarity, and there's no going back.

THE MOMENT OF LIBERATION

Rose's abusive cousin lived in Oregon, and she decided it made the most sense to do her carefrontation by phone. "Economically and time-wise, it would cost too much to go, so I called him and made an appointment to talk. When I started therapy, I broke off contact with him, but I told him someday I would call him. I hadn't spoken to him in four years.

"I had done so much writing with my little girl leading up to this, and there was all this uncertainty I hadn't felt before. At the moment I was supposed to call him, I was thinking, 'Why has there been all this fear?' In my writing, I found that I was doubting things I'd never questioned, and I couldn't figure out why. But when I talked to him I knew.

"Most of my interactions with him had been in Spanish, so the night before the carefrontation, I wrote a version of my letter in Spanish, and that's what I read him. He listened to the whole thing, and then he denied everything. He said I made it all up, that it never happened, and he told me I must've fantasized about him when I was a little kid. I was shaking and crying as I listened, but I was able to be very clear in my truth. I realized that it didn't matter what he said, because *I* knew the truth.

"I said, 'Are you sure you do not remember even one incident?' and he said, 'I don't recall anything. That never happened.'

"So I said, 'Thank you for listening to my letter. My request is that you don't contact me ever again. I don't want to be part of your life, and I don't want you to be part of mine. I hope you respect that. I sincerely wish you a good life, because I know I will have a great one.'

"It was very clear to me that my little girl knew he was going to deny it, and that's why she was writing and letting me know—to prepare me. I feel happy and sad for my little kid, because I know she would've wished it would be a kumbaya moment, that he would've said, 'I'm sorry I hurt you.' But when he denied it, I knew he was lying. No 'dream' ever affected me for thirty years. I was absolutely clear."

Rose found she was calm after the carefrontation. "I had you and my best friend and my sponsor on call in case I needed to talk," she told me, "and I was prepared to take the day off so I could be with my little girl. But I was there for her in the carefrontation, and I was able to go on about my day and do what I needed to, taking care of her and of me as a woman, and attend to my business. That's something I wouldn't have been able to do if my little girl hadn't helped me be so clear and prepared."

Today, Rose says the carefrontation was the best gift she ever gave herself. "Now," she says, "I know there's nothing in this world I can't do. When my cousin denied everything, I realized what the carefrontation was for me. It was all in that moment of telling my truth. If I ever doubt myself and say 'I can't do this,' I will think back to it. I was liberated at that moment. Whatever I do from now on, I'll do wholeheartedly, as an integrated, secure woman."

Her other two carefrontations, with each of her parents, were equally freeing for her. Her father surprised her by taking full responsibility and tearfully apologizing to her. And though her mother denied everything, the simple act of stating her truth, Rose told me, was transformative.

"Although I did not get any validation from my mom, I healed by disclosing my truth without any reservations," she said. "I felt a tremendous amount of relief after disclosing all the events that had occurred in our home. I believe the relief came from all the writing assignments and processing leading up to my carefrontation. The assignments let me become unattached to the outcome of disclosing my truth. Today, I know that my mother may never take responsibility or acknowledge that she was unable to keep me safe, yet I am able to let it go and live my life without reservations. I finally got the inner confidence and self-validation that I was searching for."

STEP NINE: WRITE TO YOUR CHILD

After you finish your carefrontation, when you get back home or to a safe place, sit down and write to your child. Thank your child for sharing his or her story with you, and with your dominant hand, ask how the child is feeling.

Use your nondominant hand to let the child respond.

Answer with your dominant hand, and in your own words, tell the child: "I will be here for you, and everything will be okay."

You are in charge now. You are the parent.

WHERE DO YOU GO FROM HERE?

What happens in your relationship with the abuser(s) or non-protector(s) will depend on how willing they are to honor your truth and offer support to you now. If you decide you want a relationship, you'll set boundaries that are safe and comfortable for your child and you. You may opt out of family gatherings, keep your meetings polite, or welcome a new kind of closeness into the relationship. Any route you choose will be based on respect and honesty.

You've lived in a haze of confusion all of your life, trying to make sense out of the senseless. Today is a new beginning, the moment you come to your life with clarity, truth, and power.

You have already made the hard choices to be on your own team, to believe and stand up for your child, and to be a good parent. Now, step-by-step, choose the path that fulfills you. Remember always to live in your truth and not the lies.

You have made a remarkable journey.

You have reclaimed your life.

14

THE FINAL STEP
Graduation

People know when they're ready to graduate into their victim-free life in the days and weeks after the carefrontation. They carry courage in their bodies, where there used to be only fear and resentment, and their stories of abuse belong to the past. Their lives are no longer run by the child, and they live in the present.

"I started to see things changing," Steven said, as he looked back at the process. "I was present in a way I'd never been before. I'm finally in possession of myself and my life now. I wasn't conscious most of the time that I responded to situations with childlike reactions. I couldn't see it. But I'm no longer afraid of being abused, which I discovered I had been my whole life. I stand up for myself because I know that I'm an adult, not the poor kid hiding under the bed. I don't jump when my boss raises his voice, or shy away from telling people what I think because they might get upset. I used to feel like I couldn't move without something blowing up. Now I can take care of myself.

"Life just gets simpler," he told me. "There's no drama. It's quiet inside me. It's nice. And that just starts to come when you stop re-acting to the past instead of being in the present."

When it's time to graduate, there's no sea of uncried tears left inside you, no stab of shame when you talk about what happened to you as a child, no compulsion to hide. There's no numbness or denial, either. Your story is your story—you own it, and it no longer owns you.

When people who have graduated talk about their lives, it's striking to see how often they refer to joy and freedom and feeling a real, honest closeness to other people they'd never known was possible.

Once you've integrated the wisdom of your child and the One Who Knows, you have the tools to act instead of react. Carrying those tools with you and using them becomes an everyday habit that makes you feel consciously proactive when life gets stressful or confusing. Challenges and disappointments don't stop coming just because you've done this work on yourself, though it's tempting to fantasize that there will be a magical "happily ever after." Instead, you know how to keep the adult in charge, and protect the child's well-being.

"In my younger days, before I did this work, I would forever go into jobs or situations and be sexually harassed but not know how to keep myself safe or understand what was going on. That doesn't happen anymore," said Grace, the math teacher who had been physically and sexually abused by her stepbrother and stepfa-ther. "Just the other day, someone came to repair my dryer. He kept coming on to me, saying stuff like, 'We could make a special deal if you want.'

"The old me would have said, 'I don't understand what he's doing.' My little girl taught me that that's something I always used to do. My mom never believed me when I talked about the abuse—she'd always say, 'You must be mistaken, honey.' But the new me listened to the fear and knew what to do. I thought, 'I don't feel safe. I need to get this guy out immediately, cancel the service, and complain about him.' And that's what I did. That's the ongoing work of reparenting my kid in my current life. Keeping her safe. Keeping the adult in charge. I don't talk to her in writing as much as I used to, but when I feel myself getting upset, I absolutely remember to check in with her."

Pausing to find out what's behind unsettled feelings becomes second nature.

"I was going through a work transition," Mia, a stage manager, told me, "and was feeling very out of sorts. I didn't know why, so I did right hand/left hand with the One Who Knows and my little girl. My little girl was feeling stuck with my boss, like I was as a child, and praying that someone above him would swoop in and save me. I could see how I had given up all my power as an adult. So I called my boss's boss and said, 'I know there is an opportunity for a promotion, and I'm ready for it. You can see by the work I've done over the past months that I'm more than qualified.'

"I wanted a promotion, I knew I wasn't going to be considered, and now I'm getting it—because I could ask. Before this work where I took on my past in such a gutsy way, I don't know if I could've asked for the promotion. The old me would've been too scared about how my boss would react.

"But now, whenever I stop to ask myself what I need, I can get past the paralysis of 'This isn't fair' and the injustice of it all, and do what I need to. Like the hero we've been working for me to become!"

A whole series of inner shifts, in the following list, make it possible to graduate from being a victim and to experience the kind of adulthood Steven, Grace, and Mia describe. These shifts flow from all the work you've done, and from everything the carefrontation and its aftermath have taught you. They'll look familiar to you—we've been working on them a long time. Check in now, and see where you stand.

ARE YOU READY TO GRADUATE INTO ADULTHOOD?

Look at the following checklist and mark what is true for you:

☐ I've completed my carefrontation.

☐ I believe my child and the truth of what happened to me.

☐ I have stopped making excuses for the people who have harmed me.

☐ It is no longer acceptable for me to betray or compromise myself to anyone.

☐ My story no longer owns me or runs my life.

☐ I am 100 percent on my team, and I am the one responsible for myself, my life, and my child.

☐ I regularly check in with myself, especially when I feel unsettled or upset. I respond to situations now, instead of just reacting.

☐ I live my life in truth and with integrity.

☐ I am becoming more and more the person I was meant to be.

You're ready to graduate when you see yourself distinctly in this mirror. You may be here now, and you may know there is more for you to do. Wherever you stand, I'm extremely proud that you've come this far. I know what I've asked you to do in this book may rank among the most difficult undertakings of your life. You are a true hero.

Following, you'll find the final exercises I'd like you to do to fulfill your graduation. They're letters to be written from the person you are today to your abuser(s) and parents, and to your child. Take them on when you're able to answer a confident yes to all the statements in the previous checklist.

Don't rush to complete these final steps. When I work with clients individually and in my groups, we often schedule a letter a week, rather than trying to get them done in one quick swoop. Writing these letters, and comparing them to the ones you wrote when we started out, will give you a clear sense of how much progress you've made and show you how much your inner landscape has changed. The basement door is open, you know how to release the old emotions, and you and your child can stand in the bright light of the present, safe and free.

ASSIGNMENT 1: Write a Letter From the Person You Are Today to the Person Who Started This Journey

When you look back on your first writing assignments, you'll see a person who was scared, angry, and probably extremely doubtful about the prospects of healing. Write to that person, sharing both your compassion for who you were and the joy of saying good-bye to the pain you thought would be with you forever. I'd like to show you several examples of this letter from people you've come to know in the book because I find them so inspiring, and I know you will too.

Rose looked back with great appreciation for what it had taken to reach the end of her journey. Here's what she wrote:

Dear Rose,

Welcome to the beginning of your healing process. You have been searching for a solution for many years and at many places. Today you walked into a solution that you longed for. I know you're filled with fear, and this new journey is not going to be easy. At times it will appear unbearable. What I know about you is that you are a strong, courageous woman and will draw on those traits many times to keep you true to yourself. You no longer need to run the show. You get to surrender and do the work. I know you're afraid to feel but please allow yourself to have your feelings. You are an amazing and talented woman. It is time to let your star shine bright and start your new healed life.

Amen!

With love,

Rose

Steven chronicled and celebrated his growth:

A hearty and heartfelt welcome to the man I am today! A welcome to the man who stands up for himself, who no longer needs to let everyone know he is okay. I know I am okay today, and I welcome the knowing.

I am no longer a victim of those painful cravings "to be approved of" and "to be accepted." I approve of myself, and I accept the man I am today. I welcome "me," the man I am today.

I dream today. I know my wants, and I take the actions necessary to get what I want and accomplish my dreams. I am a man who welcomes success and does not fear failure. There is no failure anymore. There are only results produced. I am a man whose thoughts and actions are congruent, and when they are not, the man I am today owns the tools to make the adjustments needed, because my emotional sobriety is as important to me as being physically fit and spiritually sound. The man I am today cherishes and honors and protects my emotional sobriety. I no longer abandon myself or hand myself over to others. I take excellent care of my little kid. I do not serve him up to anyone. I listen to him. I protect him with the power of a father who truly loves his child and shows it by his actions every day.

The man I am today can admit when I am wrong and make prompt amends. I meet my obligations and responsibilities. I am able to experience gratitude. I reach out to others who need my help. I am no longer afraid to take on new challenges and more responsibilities.

I embrace the man I am today. I am open to attain more knowledge and higher wisdom. I am not afraid to love God. I am willing to be the man I want to be and who my little kid wants me to be: full of love, compassion, toughness, loyalty, trustworthiness, gentleness, patience, kindness, fierceness, and dedication.

Mike spoke to his "old" self in a voice full of love, acceptance, and gratitude:

Dear old me,

Parts of you still exist but parts of you are but a memory.

First, thank you for being so brave and willing in the beginning. Without that courage I wouldn't be here today. We are forever changed thanks to your efforts and this world, our world, is another place because of you.

I want you to know that I don't blame you. In fact, I love you more today than I ever have. I have finally faced the pains so deep and see clearly that you saved us. You kept our head above water in the scariest of storms and through it all remained a person who people loved to love.

Today I love you. I love me. I know you didn't have the tools to protect yourself and that's why we were always running. We don't have to run anymore.

I know that when you looked in the mirror you saw shame and guilt for other people's actions that you truly were the victim of. Today I see a beautiful man inside and out. Always working to be better, but not afraid to stumble or be less than perfect.

We never have to feel ashamed of our fantasies. We can embrace our sexuality and use it to enhance our life and our partnership.

You were never bad, and today I know that idea is gone. We no longer stay up at night worrying about what the next day holds for us. That's what we've always longed for, it's what we've worked for, and it's what we deserve.

We love today with abandon and leave the future in the universe's hands.

Today you and I, my friend, are on a beautifully wild ride rather than a nightmare. Yes, those days are gone. And just so you know without any doubt, I'll say it again. We deserve this life. We deserve this joy. I love you.

Me

ASSIGNMENT 2: Write Letters to Your Abusers and Non-protectors From the Powerful Person You Are Today

Write separate letters to your mother, your father, and to anyone who abused you. Tell your truth with the strength and wisdom you've worked so hard to earn.

Here's the letter Steven wrote to his non-protective mother:

Dear Mom:

You should see me now!

The last thing you said to me after I carefronted you was, "I hope your life goes better." Actually, that was the only thing you said to me. Today, my life doesn't just go better. Today, I have a life—despite the fact that you never took responsibility for not taking care of me and for neglecting my well-being when I was a child. Little Stevie needed you, and you weren't there.

Today, I am a man who is an advocate for Stevie. I am the man who protects him and listens to him. I contain him when he is anxious. I hold him when he is scared. I am a man who has now taken responsibility for my life, and I have cast off all the shame and given it back to those it really belongs to.

I take responsibility for my actions today, and I let no one off the hook, nor do I protect or cover for anyone who has hurt Stevie or any other children.

I am a success today! I am respected. I am an excellent actor and a good writer with the inner life of a lion!

I have broken the chain of silence and abuse, and I am damn proud of it! I am dedicated and loyal, and I have a passionate soul. I earn more money than I have ever earned in my life, and my career gets better every day. I am not afraid of the power inside me, and I continue to dig down even deeper and mine my soul for all the treasure I can find.

My life is getting bigger and better, and I welcome it. I can handle it, because I am an empowered child of God and I know it! I am a man today, a real man with feelings I can identify. I refuse to be numb or settle for a life in a low-grade depression. I have stepped into a higher plane inside a whole new empowered life.

Mom, you should see me now!

Your son,

Stevie & Steven

The sense of inner safety and power that Rose felt after her carefrontations left her with a new compassion for her parents, which she expressed in her letter to her mother:

Dear Mom,

I held on to resentment for so many years. I resented you for not protecting me and not keeping me safe. The anger and resentment I felt was hurting me and dictated a lot of actions I took. Thank God that I was able to join and participate in group therapy. I learned how to finally cut the umbilical cord and establish a healthy relationship with you. I was able to let go of all the anger and resentment and look straight at you and speak my truth. I am not afraid to tell you how I feel and how it was your responsibility to keep me safe when I was a child. I can hold you accountable for the lack of actions on your part to keep me safe while still being a loving daughter. I can speak firmly and confidently. I am no longer in fear of losing your love or seeking your approval. I am comfortable speaking my truth and no longer ashamed. I love you Mom, and can only hope and pray that one day you find the same freedom that I have today.

Love,
Rose

Her letter to her cousin was succinct and clear. She was powerful, and no longer his victim:

Richard,

For many years I kept it a secret that you sexually abused me for fear of being called a liar and because I thought my dad would kill you. What you did to me was a criminal act and harmed me. Today I realize that it does not matter if you admit or take responsibility for your actions in sexually abusing me. It is enough for me to know my truth and be able to speak my truth. I am free of all shame or guilt. I hope we never cross paths again.

Rose

With the same kind pride, confidence, and clarity you see in these letters, write to your abuser(s)/non-protector(s). Tell them what you most need to say about who you are now, and how you see them today. Note that your letters do not have to be long to carry the certainty and understandings you now possess.

ASSIGNMENT 3: Write a Letter to Your Child

In this final letter, give your child your love, your thanks, and your vision of your future together. Be sure the child knows that from now on, you'll be together and that you will provide love and care. Here's what Rose told her little girl:

Dear Little Rose,

Sweetie, we have come a long way together. At the beginning of this journey, I did not know you. One day at a time I have been getting to know you. I have shared many painful memories and have grown to love you unconditionally. I celebrate who you are and am looking forward to spending the rest of our lives together. I am looking forward to creating many wonderful memories and exploring the world with you. My promise to you is that I will be here to guide you, protect you, and nurture you. I will be patient, kind, and loving. We will try new things together and participate in many adventures.

You will be my companion. We will laugh and cry together.

All I ask from you is to continue speaking up and be authentic. You are a beautiful, intelligent, and courageous little girl. You are a shining, bright star. You no longer need to be silent. You can sing, skip around, or just be. You are a wonderful human being. No need to be small. Let your star shine my little one. I love you dearly.

Your mom,
Rose

ASSIGNMENT 4: Read All These Letters Aloud

Stand up and read your letters to a therapist, your partner or spouse, or someone who has supported you on this journey. How does it feel to speak and hear these words? It's hard to miss the love the writers of the letters in the preceding pages feel for themselves and the child within them. Do you see that kind of love in your own letters? If not, and particularly if your letters sound as though they were written by someone still trapped inside the point of view of a victim, write them again.

If the words you wrote sound true to you and reflect the empowered adult you are today, then I say: *Congratulations on your graduation!*

Please turn the page and sign the marriage certificate you'll find there. I give graduates a marriage certificate, not a diploma, to reflect that in graduating, you are making a commitment to yourself for the rest of your life. I want you to promise that you'll take care of yourself, not be a victim, and live a fulfilling life.

I wish you the best of everything—love, peace, and great joy. You deserve them, and you have earned them.

CERTIFICATE OF MARRIAGE

Because I am the only person I will have a relationship with all of my life, I choose:

- To love, honor, and cherish myself
- To treat myself with kindness and patience
- To live in my truth, always
- To trust that I am enough, just the way I am
- To be there for myself, no matter what, for the rest of my life
- To always nurture my mind, my heart, and my spirit
- To continue to grow, develop, and follow my own path

This is my commitment to myself and my child on

_____

[date]

_____

[Signature]

You are amazing. Congratulations! You are free.

AFTERWORD

Everyone you've met in these pages has *recovered* from childhood abuse. Today, these men and women are unfurling dreams and talents that had been consumed by their pasts, and building lives they had once thought they'd never have. While they face all the daily issues everyone does, they come at them through a solid, healthy core—as adults.

"Life now is pretty low-key," Mike said. "It's funny because I thought that after graduation, I wouldn't experience feelings of being overwhelmed or sad. I had a rosy picture of what it was supposed to be like, and then I realized life is life, and that was a fairy tale. But I can handle things now. But today I look in the mirror and I love that person looking back at me.

"What remains most important to me is knowing what to do with my feelings. If I find myself feeling upset, I want to find out where that feeling is coming from and address that. I don't do much writing to my little boy unless I'm going through something, but I do a lot of meditating and praying, and I continue my conversations with my child as I think about him. I keep his picture on my desk at work, and I look at him all day long to be sure he's okay. It seemed like an impossible task at the beginning, and now it's second nature."

The road rage and sexual acting out are gone, he says, and his relationship with his partner has never been better. They're now the fathers of twin baby girls.

Grace talks about having a new kind of resilience that has made her more open to life. "I went from being incapable of talking about my feelings on any level to having the capacity to allow my heart to be broken, because that's part of life. If you're human, your heart will be broken many times by love or disappointment. But what makes my life rich and full is allowing my heart to open and knowing I'll be safe even in heartbreak. I have a choice: I can be emotionally aware and fully alive or be a bitter, closed-off human being. I choose the former. I've never been happier. I know how to root down into what I am and not escape. The warrior part of me can stand up and speak the truth."

I'd like to end this book with Rose, who experienced some of the most intense abuse I've seen, and who, as you've seen in these pages, worked with great dedication to earn her freedom from her past. Though she does not consider herself to be a writer, and was dubious about committing to a process that involves so much written work, she wanted to heal more than she wanted to resist. Here's her view from the other side of recovery:

"There are no toxic people in my life anymore," she says. "I don't have superficial relationships with anyone, not even with my clients. My personal relationships are very deep, of substance. I'm in a committed relationship with a man, and I had never been in one before this. He's loving, caring, and supportive, which is quite a switch from before. I was only attracting predators, alcoholics, and men who were unkind, unloving, and verbally abusive. I have no one in my life like that anymore.

"I am happy—I have peace, serenity, and tranquility. For the first twenty-five years of my life, I was in a war. For the next ten years, I was in a war in my mind. Now, for the next thirty or forty years, I have peace. I don't know what I will do next—I feel like

I'm in the toddler years of my life. But whatever I choose will be awesome, amazing, and perfect for Little Rose.

"Sharing my journey is my way of paying it forward," she said. "I got my life back. I hope other people can do the same."

Take courage from every story you saw in this book, and every discovery you've made along the way.

Trust yourself. You have everything you need within you.

ACKNOWLEDGMENTS

I am grateful to the many people, including but not limited, to the following:

My agent, Margret McBride, the Margret McBride Literary Agency, for believing in me from the beginning and her associate Faye Atchison, for her hard work and for always being responsive to my needs.

My publisher, Judith Regan, and my editor, Kathryn Huck, for their enthusiasm and care in shepherding this book.

Elyse Resch, MS, RDN, for her support, advice, and calming and dedicated presence throughout the writing of this book.

My clients, who so graciously gave their personal stories to this book, in order to help others heal, as they did.

All of my clients throughout the years who have allowed me to be a part of their healing journey.

Tracey Landworth

Arlene Drake is a pioneer in the field of childhood abuse and trauma recovery. She has long been a passionate crusader for victims' rights and has been featured in media outlets including the *Los Angeles Times*, *People* magazine, *Newsweek*, *USA Today*, and ABC *World News Tonight*. She is a member of both the California Association of Marriage and Family Therapists (CAMFT) and the Clinical Hypnosis Association. Drake lives and works in the Los Angeles area.